How
TO BE A
Praying
Mom

How
TO BE A
Praying
Mom

JEANNIE ST. JOHN TAYLOR

Unless otherwise indicated, all Scripture quotations are taken from the *Holy Bible*, New
Living Translation, copyright © 1996. Used by permission of Tyndale House
Publishers, Inc., Wheaton, Illinois 60189. All rights reserved.

Scripture quotations marked (NIV) are taken from the HOLY BIBLE, NEW INTER-
NATIONAL VERSION®. NIV®. Copyright © 1973, 1978, 1984 by International
Bible Society. Used by permission of Zondervan Publishing House. All rights reserved.

Scripture quotations marked (NKJV) are taken from the *New King James Version of the Bible*.
Copyright © 1979, 1980, 1982, and 1990 by Thomas Nelson, Inc., Publishers. Used
by permission of Thomas Nelson, Inc. All rights reserved.

Printed in the United States of America

ISBN 1-56563-651-1

Third printing ---- October, 2002

Cover design by Richmond & Williams, Nashville, Tennessee
Interior design and typesetting by Reider Publishing Services, San Francisco, California
Edited by Judy Bodmer, Mary McNeil, and Deneen Sedlack

Library of Congress Cataloging-in-Publication Data

Taylor, Jeannie, 1945–
    How to be a praying mom / Jeannie St. John Taylor.
        p. cm.
    ISBN 1-56563-651-1 (cloth)
    1. Mothers–Religious life. 2. Prayer. I. Title.

BV4529.18.T39 2001
248.3'2'0852–dc21

                                                           2001024400

*For my parents, Gladys and Clare St. John, who still pray for me daily
And for my children, Ty, Tori, and Tevin, for whom I pray constantly*

"Prayer does not equip us for greater works.
Prayer is the greater work. Prayer is *the* battle."

— OSWALD CHAMBERS

Acknowledgments

I want the people who helped with this project to know my heart toward them. Several godly women poured the gift of prayer into its pages as I wrote. Those prayers made this book what it is. I am deeply grateful.

Barbara Martin, my prayer and writing partner for years, read through the manuscript twice, critiquing and offering invaluable help.

Judy Bodmer, Mary McNeil, and Deneen Sedlack, editors par excellence, knew how to tweak my words without changing their intent. Every correction they suggested was precisely right.

Dan Penwell organized the flow of the book, read through it numerous times as he worked to craft it, and kept me posted on its progress. His flexibility and encouragement made my job easy. I am humbled to call him my friend.

And last, my husband, Ray, who loves to help people, cooked all the meals and loaded the dishwasher to allow more time for me to write.

Contents

Introduction

*Y*ou love your children. You might even love them enough to give your life for them. You want them to grow strong and healthy, to live successful happy lives, to love the Lord with all their strength and might, to live peacefully, to have all their physical and emotional needs met, to marry well and never suffer the pain of divorce.

But most of those things are beyond your control. They depend on circumstances, other people, and your own children's choices. What can you do about them? Is there any way you can insure a better life for your children?

Yes. You can pray for them daily.

Though there are no absolute guarantees, prayer has the power to work miracles. It can

- reach into stubborn, rebellious hearts and completely reverse attitudes
- heal damaged emotions and memories
- protect from physical injury

- direct your children toward healthy choices
- break the bonds of addiction
- comfort the brokenhearted
- pull a child from a coma

Prayer is the greatest gift you can give your children. It can prevent much heartache and place them in a position where God can bless them. It can reach out to touch and protect them even when you don't know where they are or what they are doing.

But prayer can be exhausting work, and only one person loves your children enough to bless them through prayer day after day, week after week, year after year.

You.

If you don't pray for them, who will?

That's a scary thought, isn't it? You *must* pray for them. It's the most important job you will ever hold. Even if you are the CEO of a large corporation or a surgeon saving lives, praying for your children is more important. It is your first responsibility. CEOs and doctors can be replaced. Your prayers cannot.

But do you sometimes feel as though your prayers are inadequate? Does your mind wander when you try to pray? Are you tempted to quit praying? Do you wonder if you are praying enough? Or even if you are really praying?

If so, stop right now and tell the Lord about it. Confess your flaws, your failures, your sins . . . and ask him to forgive you. He will.

How to Use This Book

As you read this book, let it

- show you how to pray into your children the foundation from which God can lead them into his specific will for their lives
- model how to funnel God's attitudes, wisdom, and blessings into their hearts and lives through prayer
- inspire you to pray God's rules for successful living into your children
- encourage you to keep praying

Do this each day:

- Set a regular time and place to meet with the Lord, even though this may be difficult for moms with jobs or young children.
- Spend a few minutes examining your heart and asking God to forgive any sin you find there.
- Read one or two sections from part one of this book. Stop as soon as you feel drawn to prayer.

- Find today's calendar date, then turn to the section of written prayers and pray the one whose number matches that date. Continue praying as the Lord leads.
- After you have prayed, cut out the designated prayer card with the corresponding number from the back of the book. Put it where you can refer to it often—in your wallet, on the bathroom mirror, or in the car. Let it constantly remind you how to pray for your children that day.

Section One

Prayer Thoughts from a Praying Mom

Grandma's Heritage of Daily Prayer

I suppose I was six or seven the afternoon I crawled up into the overstuffed chair by my grandmother's bedroom door and reached for the multicolored afghan draped over the back. Wrapping it around me like a warm hug, I wiggled into its comfort to wait for Grandma.

Over by the brown enamel oil stove, three cousins pushed toy trucks across the flowered carpet. Uncle Keith snoozed open-mouthed on the couch, while murmurs of adult after-dinner conversation drifted in from the dining room.

The squeak of the wood cook stove door told me Grandma was still in the kitchen, but she wouldn't be there long. The clock registered one minute until three—and Grandma prayed at exactly three every afternoon. She wouldn't let anything lure her from her daily prayer routine.

The clock began to strike. *Bong! Bong!* Brisk footsteps crossed the kitchen linoleum, and Grandma appeared in the doorway. *Bong!*

Hurrying through the living room, she bent to kiss the top of my head before she entered her bedroom and closed the door behind her.

The weight of the clothes hanging on the back of the door pulled it ajar, and I rested my chin on the arm of the chair to watch. She knelt beside her bed, clasped her hands in prayer, and began mentioning each of her children and grandchildren by name. With "loud cries" she lifted her spirit and voice to the Lord—totally oblivious to the fact that anyone else was in the house.

Uncle Keith continued to snore. The cousins revved their trucks and ran them over a pillow. Conversation in the dining room continued without a pause. Everyone was so used to Grandma's daily prayers that they barely noticed. Except me. I loved listening for my name.

My parents tell me that from the time Grandma found out my mother was pregnant, she prayed for me. Every single day. Never missed. Down through my life, whenever I faced problems, I remembered my grandma praying for me. I knew she wouldn't forget. It was such a comfort. The knowledge that she prayed always brought back the same warm secure feeling that enveloped me the day I listened by her bedroom door.

I felt that way even when I wasn't walking with the Lord.

I wish I could tell you I never faltered. I wish I could say my grandmother's prayer kept me from slipping into sin. But it wouldn't be true. Sadly, Grandma died when I was in my mid-twenties—still away from the Lord. She probably thought all her prayers had been useless.

But they weren't.

I am certain her prayers played a large part in bringing me back to the Lord. There is no way to express how grateful I am for them.

This is why I felt the urgent need to continue the prayer tradition with my own children. If prayer was so powerful it could pull me back into the arms of Jesus, how could I not offer the gift of prayer to them?

So from the time I found out I was pregnant, I prayed for each of my children every day. When the kids were little, my prayers didn't sound much like Grandma's. It was nearly impossible to stick to a routine, and the only "alone time" I found was in the shower. So I prayed silently as I ironed and cooked and picked up toys. As the kids got older, the bulk of my prayer time took place while I waited in the car at soccer and baseball practices.

My children are grown now, and my prayer times have changed. Because I have more time to myself, I am able to schedule a set time and place for prayer. And lately, I often find myself praying out loud. Speaking aloud helps me concentrate. It also keeps me awake if I feel sleepy!

Praying for my children is the most important job I've ever had— or ever will have. I think they need my prayers more than ever now.

I will continue to pray for them every single day until I die.

Just like Grandma.

Do I Have to Kneel and Close My Eyes?

My grandma St. John knelt at her bedside in Michigan and closed her eyes when she prayed. Grandma Perry ran the aisles at tent meetings in Kentucky, shouting praises to the Lord with her eyes wide open. My father stood behind his pulpit praying for his spiritual children. I sit in a rocking chair with my hands raised in worship, praying for my kids. My friend Cherie walks her dog as she prays for hers.

Moms often teach young children to pray with their eyes closed and their hands folded reverently.

So . . . what is the correct position to assume when you pray? What does the Bible say?

- Jesus "looked up to heaven" and prayed while he reclined at a table (see John 17:1).
- In Gethsemane, Jesus "knelt down and prayed" (see Luke 22:41).

- While standing at Lazarus's tomb, Jesus "looked up to heaven" and prayed (see John 11:41).
- King David "sat before the Lord and prayed" (see 1 Chron. 18:16).
- The seraphim hovered over the Lord saying, "Holy, holy, holy . . ." (see Isa. 6:3).
- Moses "lay prostrate before the Lord" for forty days and nights (see Deut. 9:17).
- Solomon "knelt down and lifted his hands toward heaven" (see 2 Chron. 6:13).
- Elijah "walked up to the altar and prayed" (see 1 Kings 18:36).
- Elijah "fell to the ground and prayed" (see 1 Kings 18:42).
- Hezekiah, while lying in bed, "turned his face to the wall and prayed" (see Isa. 38:2).
- Joshua and other leaders "tore their clothing . . . threw dust on their heads, and bowed down facing the ark" (see Josh. 7:6).
- King David "danced before the Lord with all his might" (see 2 Sam. 6:14).
- Paul and Barnabas prayed with feet clamped in stocks (see Acts 16:24).

All the physical prayer positions in the Bible seem to have one or two things in common: either the position is a natural response to the emotion of the person praying, or the position is forced on the person. David danced when he experienced joy. Moses lay facedown, grieving. Paul prayed in stocks because he had no other choice. God seems to accept any body position when you pray.

So when you pray for your children, fold your hands, open or close your eyes, stand, sit, kneel, dance, fall on your face, rock the baby, bend over as you change a diaper, or sit cross-legged on the floor at a gymnastics meet. Pray in whatever position is necessary.

Just keep praying for your kids.

The Very Best Prayer

I could read the disappointment in my oldest son's posture as he leaned on his crutches by the javelin pit. Track was Ty's favorite sport; he especially loved throwing the javelin. But a knee injury had ended his first college track season. So instead of spending his Saturday competing in a college meet, he stood by a high school track waiting to watch his little brother throw.

Ty nudged his sister and pointed to the runway where Tevin, a high school sophomore, stood poised with his javelin at shoulder height. Tori stopped chatting as she and Ty fastened their attention on their younger brother. Tevin raised the javelin and began his side-stepping run down the asphalt. I could see Ty's body tighten in anticipation. I held my breath.

The javelin shot from Tevin's hand and soared into the air. As if in slow motion, it rose higher, then flattened out for a several seconds before it descended. It landed point down near one of the farthest white lines. A great throw! The crowd roared. I cheered wildly.

Down by the runway, Ty celebrated—waving his crutches in the air and hopping around on his good leg while holding onto his sister's shoulder.

The stands quieted, waiting for the officials to stretch out the tape and measure the throw. "One hundred seventy-nine feet and six inches." No one else in our high school league could match that throw. Everyone exploded into cheers again.

Except me.

Conflicting feelings churned inside me. I hadn't expected the throw to be *that* good. Even though I was thrilled for Tevin, and I could see Ty clapping him on the back excitedly, I felt sad for Ty. His brother, three years younger, had thrown a few inches farther than Ty's best throw. It was bound to make Ty a little envious. Wasn't it?

I asked him later, "Ty, didn't it make you feel a little bad?" I didn't say, "When your younger brother beat you," out loud. But we both knew what I meant.

He stared at me with amazement. "Why would it? Tevin's success doesn't take anything from me."

I could tell he was genuinely shocked by the question. He was thrilled for his brother. There was absolutely no sibling rivalry between them.

None.

But it hadn't always been that way.

I remember glancing out the window of the cabin we rented one vacation shortly before Tori turned six and Tevin five, and witnessing my daughter unexpectedly pummel Tevin with her fists. Before I could rush to his defense, she whirled, burst through the door, and ran toward me yelling, "Tevin hit me!"

Another time, at the beach, four-year-old Tevin ran to me in tears, his blue striped sweater and jeans soaked with ocean water. He threw his arms around my legs, sobbing, "Ty twicked me into da wada!" He looked and sounded so cute I was tempted to smile. But I didn't. I knew the cold water soaking his shoes and pants was building hatred between the two brothers.

As they got older, the fights came more often. Dissension zapped like a continuous electric current among the three of them. I prayed without ceasing. They fought without ceasing.

I made them memorize verses: "It is to a man's honor to avoid strife."

I worried in prayer.

I disciplined them.

The fighting got worse. I had hoped my three children would be best friends. But instead, they were enemies.

Everything came to a head three days before the summer vacation of Ty's fifth-grade year. I was heading for the washing machine with a basket of laundry when I heard angry voices in the driveway.

Fighting.

Again.

I couldn't stand it any more! I couldn't stand them. How could I endure another summer like this? Dropping my laundry, I flung myself spread-eagle across the top of my washing machine and prayed the very best prayer a person can pray: "HELP!"

I sprawled there praying out loud—crying out loud—for some time. "Please help me, Lord. You're my only hope. Please stop the fighting because I can't. I don't have any idea how to make them stop. And I can't stand it any more." When I finally finished begging, there was silence. I crept to the window and looked outside. The three kids were playing peacefully in the front yard.

Fighting was never a problem again. I don't know why God chose that particular day to answer my prayer. But I know he answered.

And I know it was a miracle.

And I know I'm no one special.

He'll work miracles for your kids, too.

Note: A few weeks after Tevin threw the javelin, Ty, his knee mended, competed in the NAIA national college track meet. He far exceeded his own best throw to win tenth in the nation. God does bless.

You Must Pray for This

The first thing every mother *must* pray for is the salvation of her children. Unless our children accept Jesus into their hearts, their lives will be wasted. They may become the most popular star athletes at school, accrue billions in the stock market, or win the presidency, but if they refuse to follow the Lord, they will suffer emotionally in this life. And eventually end up in hell, languishing in eternal loneliness and pain.

But if they accept the Lord and obey him

- he will be the firm foundation on which they build their lives
- he will bless them
- they can ask for wisdom—and receive it
- they can avoid the pain caused by sinful choices
- instead of stewing in confusion, they will know right from wrong
- they never need be crippled by guilt, because God forgives every sin
- he will actually help them grow as a result of trials and trouble

- he will lead them into good works that benefit many
- after they die, he will reward them in heaven
- and they will be reunited with you

So pray for the salvation of your children. It's never too soon or too late to start. Just don't stop until they know Jesus as their Savior. Keep praying until they ask him to forgive their sins.

Pray John 3:16: "God, thank you for loving the world so much you sent your Son to die for us. Help my children believe in you."

Then start praying through Romans. "Lord, I know sin will bring death to my children. But you have offered them the free gift of eternal life. Help them accept it" (see Rom. 6:23). "Help my children confess with their mouths that Jesus is Lord. Help them to believe that God raised him from the dead. Save their souls" (see Rom. 10:9–10).

Keep on praying. Never quit. Never give up hope. My grandmother died thinking her prayers for me hadn't been answered. But they had. It just took thirty years. I've heard of people who prayed for forty years before God answered prayers for the salvation of their loved ones. But he answered.

Believe God will save your children. After all, why wouldn't he? He loves them even more than you do. And your continued prayers open the path for them to accept him.

Night Praises

When my children were young, it seemed I never found chunks of time when I could pray in solitude. I shot requests heavenward as I picked up toys and cooked dinner, but I couldn't seem to find a time to get off by myself and really pray. The only alone time I could grab was in the shower, and even then I could see little Tevin through the foggy glass, upturned bottle in his right hand, left palm pressed against the shower door.

Exhausted at night, I fell asleep the minute I closed my eyes to pray, too tired to bless God or pray for my children. I felt so guilty . . . until one night I asked, "Lord, please allow my spirit to worship and pray as I sleep."

I didn't know if it was possible, but I knew God does impossible things. I knew the Holy Spirit lives inside me. And I knew James says, "The reason you don't have what you want is that you don't ask God for it" (James 4:2).

So I asked.

That night, every time I woke up—I was praying for my children. The Holy Spirit within me remembered my babies to the Father as I slept!

Aaron Prayers

When my oldest son left for afternoon kindergarten, I panicked. I knew he needed prayer more than ever before, but for the first time in his life, I couldn't keep a close eye on him to know how to pray. I couldn't watch him at school to see if he got along with his peers. I couldn't know when he felt lonely or sad because someone picked on him. I couldn't see when his little hand couldn't form letters easily. How could I ask God to meet needs I didn't know about?

Finally, I decided to put my other two children down for naps and pray Aaron prayers every day when he left for school.

God revealed the concept of Aaron prayers to me one time as I read Exodus. God appointed Aaron, Moses's older brother, to represent God's children by carrying their names before God in the tabernacle. Exodus 28 details the "clothing with a purpose" God designed for Aaron to wear as he entered the Most Holy Place to meet with God.

Attached to the front of Aaron's patterned turban with a blue cord, a large gold medallion rested on his forehead. The words engraved on it declared Aaron's importance to God. They read, "set apart as holy to the Lord."

Over a blue robe, two large onyx stones set in gold filigree joined the front and back pieces of his apronlike priestly ephod at the shoulders with cords of pure gold. I imagine the stones flat and palm sized, like the shoulder boards on a modern military uniform. Polished to a reflective shine, they were engraved with the names of the tribes of Israel. God wanted Aaron to "carry these names before the Lord as a constant reminder" for him to protect and bless them (see Exod. 28:12).

I thought, "Aha!" as I read those words. "I'm God's priest today. And God wants me to constantly bring the names of my children to him."

For Aaron, the names of God's children were repeated on the nine-inch-square chestpiece he wore over his heart. Twelve gemstones set in gold marched across the chestpiece in four rows, sparkling all the colors of the rainbow. Engraved with graceful letters on each stone was the name of one tribe of Israel. "In this way, Aaron [carried] the names of the tribes of Israel on the chestpiece over his heart when he [went] into the presence of the Lord in the Holy Place. Thus, the Lord [was] reminded of his [children] continually" (Exod. 28:29).

I can visualize the stones as Aaron drew aside the curtain of the Most Holy Place. Grape-sized, perfect, each gem clutched in gold, they danced a myriad of reflected colors from the flickering lights of the gold lampstand onto the linen-curtain walls of the Most Holy Place, calling out to God, "Here are the names of your children!

Remember them! Protect them! Bless them!" The light from the stones skipped across the gold posts with their silver bases, onto the golden cherubim of the ark itself.

The gold bells fastened to the hem of Aaron's blue robe tinkled as he closed the curtain. Darkness enclosed him. He bowed in silence, the thick curtains hushing all sound. The fragrance of holy incense wafted through the fabric and drifted heavenward with Aaron's adoration as the glory of God's presence lit his face. Gratitude mingled with awe for Jehovah swelled his entire being. No concerns about friends or family distracted him. As the names of his loved ones, engraved in stone, flashed and sparkled into the Father's heart from the gemstones attached to his clothing, Aaron's mind was released to concentrate fully on the Lord.

Just as Aaron entered the Most Holy Place to meet God, I have my own private place where I seek him—an antique, carved rocking chair in the corner of a pink-flowered bedroom, where photos of loved ones cluster on the dresser. When worry about my son threatened to overwhelm me, I walked to the bedroom, switched on soft worship music, and sat on the chair's needlepoint seat. Holding my hands palm up in an attitude of worship, I mentally placed my son in them and lifted him up to God.

"Ty is my precious jewel," I reminded the Lord. "I don't know what he needs, but you do. Please fill every need. Bless him."

I asked the Holy Spirit to take over the prayer burden for me. I released everything, knowing he cares about my son more than I do. His prayers are more effective than mine. I don't have to know what my son needs, because God knows—and he will fill those needs if I ask him.

Golden Bowls of Incense

I know it feels as though your prayers just—*Pop!*—disappear the instant they leave your lips. But they don't. When you breathe silent wishes for your children toward God, they don't evaporate. They aren't gone.

The fifth chapter of Revelation tells us what happens to them. It says prayers exist in the realm God inhabits with all the spiritual powers. Somehow our prayers ascend to heaven. I like to think of them as spiritual bubbles, shimmering with blues and pinks as they float upward with the mist of my children's names inside.

Right past Satan's nose.

I like to think of him ranting and raving because he despises the beauty of my prayer bubbles. I see him ducking as they pass because he's afraid of their power (they only *look* fragile), shuddering in helpless fury because he knows they will delight God.

But, of course, that is all conjecture. We don't have any idea what prayers actually look like. We only see them once in the Bible—when we tiptoe into God's throne room and kneel in worship with the apostle John. We watch as the four living beings and the twenty-four elders bow low in worship before the throne. Each one holds a harp and a golden bowl filled with incense.

And that incense is the prayers of God's people.

Your prayers can ascend to God's throne room right now! You can send anything you wish directly to God. You can tell him how much you love him. Requests for your children can exist as incense swirling around our Father. Giving him pleasure. Pleasing the God of the universe!

Mind-boggling, isn't it? It's almost too incredible to believe. But it's true. Your children can have an audience with the King of kings.

So whisper your requests along with the names of your children. They are pleasing incense to the Father. Let the incense of *your prayers* delight him. Pray right now. I can almost see God smiling with pleasure.

Does Fervent Prayer
Make a Difference?

oes fervent prayer make a difference? Evidently it does. Jesus' half brother insists that the "effective, *fervent* prayer of a righteous man avails much" (see James 5:16 NIV, italics mine).

Why would *fervent* prayer make a difference? It's a mystery no one can grasp—except moms. We get it.

The first time one of your kids hangs on your leg as you cook dinner and begs, "Please, please, please, may I have a cookie?", you understand why fervency grabs the heart of God.

You say, "Wait till dinner." But the intensity increases.

"Please . . . PLEASE!" You look down at his sweet face. It tugs at your heart. You steel yourself against it. You want to give him what he desires.

"PLEEASE . . . PUL-EEEASE!"

Eventually you cave. "Okay. Just one." There is something about zealous begging that softens the resolve of any parent. And God is our daddy. When we beg fervently, it's hard for him to say no.

I solved my tendency to accede to child harassment by making a rule that stated, "If you beg you'll never get it." But God the Father doesn't have a "no begging" rule with us. When we *reeee*ally want something, he longs to give it to us. And he will . . .

IF it is in line with his will.

Fervency doesn't guarantee a yes answer. God denied the most fervent request recorded in the Bible. In the garden, Jesus prayed with such wrenching emotion that huge drops of blood oozed from his forehead. Three times he asked God to release him from death on the cross. But it wasn't God's will. So God said no.

We know why. Jesus had to die so we could live. It seemed horrible at the time. It was horrible.

But it was God's will.

When we pray fervently it is often because we are afraid or deeply grieved. Who prays more fervently than a mom whose child is dangerously ill or not saved? We pray desperately as we watch at a child's bedside after an accident or illness. We pray with zeal as we sob over a rebellious child.

Our cries ascend to heaven. Our agonized begging catches the attention of God our Father. It tugs at his heart. He wants to comfort us by granting our heart's desires.

So wrap those arms around your Daddy's knees, look up at him, and beg for all you're worth. He'll enjoy giving you what you want—as long as it is for your best and his.

Adopt a Prayer Child

I lounged on Sylvia's front-porch steps chatting with two women I'd met just twenty minutes earlier. Sylvia leaned against a white pillar, braiding her toddler's hair. Alexis talked about the difficulties of raising her son Matthew by herself.

That reminded me of a single mother in my church who had prayed me through a problem earlier in the week. "I could *feel* her prayers," I said. "I knew exactly when she started to pray, because everything changed."

A wistful look flitted across Alexis's face. "No one ever prays for me," she said.

Her words stunned me. I didn't move. Didn't blink. Just stared at Alexis. "Surely someone prays for you," I said. It was impossible that *no one* prayed for her. Wasn't it? Doesn't everyone have someone praying? My parents still pray for me every day.

I take it for granted.

"Didn't you say your mom was a Christian?"

Alexis shrugged. "I think she is."

"Surely your mom prays for you," I said.

Alexis shook her head. "No. She's busy with her own life. No one prays for me."

I took a deep breath. What I was about to offer was a big commitment. One I never take lightly. "Tell you what, Alexis. I'll adopt you. You will be my prayer daughter and Matthew my prayer grandson. I'll pray for you every day."

"You would do that?" Her eyes grew big. "You would pray for me?"

"I will. Every day. But you need to keep in touch. I'll give you my number so you can call me whenever you need prayer. It helps me pray if I know what's going on in your life."

We talked for another thirty minutes, then parted. I haven't seen Alexis since, but I have kept my promise. Alexis is one of a number of "prayer children" I have adopted over the years. I adopt my own children's buddies. I adopt the children of my nonbelieving friends. I adopt other children and adults I am convinced no one else will pray for. Sometimes I tell them I am praying for them, sometimes I don't.

I try not to take on too many "prayer children" at a time, because they are a big responsibility. Right now I have only six. They aren't simply names I stick on a prayer list. I *commit* to pray *regularly* for my "prayer children" in the same way I do my own children.

Once every day I pray for them formally as I wait before the Lord. I ask him to reveal what he wants me to ask for them. I mention known needs. I ruminate on their personalities. Their gifts. Their flaws. I thank God for all the traits that make them individuals. I ask him to smooth out the rough points, polish them, keep their hearts right, and call them to seek him with their whole minds, hearts, and souls. I ask him to choose the perfect mate for them and keep them on the right path. I ask for his will in their lives.

Often they come to mind during the day as I work. If I feel an urgent press to pray for them, I stop and do so. Otherwise, I ask God to bless and protect them as I go about my chores.

Unlike my own children, prayer children aren't necessarily a life-long responsibility. I let God decide how long I will pray for each one. Currently, I am preparing to move the name of one prayer child to a list where I place the names of people I pray for less often. I have prayed for him daily for five years. In two weeks he will marry into a strong Christian family. Because his wife's parents will undoubtedly pray fervently for him, he won't need my prayers as much.

Because I only met Alexis one time and she didn't keep in touch, I placed her on a "less frequent" list after a year or so. Then I filled her spot with someone I saw more often.

Ask God if you should adopt a prayer child or two. Though it's a big responsibility—it's also a privilege.

Notice the Nudge

*L*ast week the name of one of my prayer children who is away at college kept buzzing my brain. Nicole. After three days I sent an e-mail to her. "Nicole, I can't get you out of my head. Do you need prayer?" By evening she responded. "Yes! I *really* need prayer right now." She proceeded to relate two major requests, and I started praying.

God, who sees everything, knew my sweet prayer child needed his help. He greatly desired to release his angels to protect her. So he nudged me with her name as a reminder to spend extra time praying for her.

Has that ever happened to you? Has the name of one of your children kept popping up unbidden as you worked during the day? You couldn't figure it out. It was weird.

More often than not, when a name keeps bugging you, the one whispering it into your ear is God. He's telling you your child needs prayer. So do it. Stop and pray fervently. Float prayers upward for her while you work. As you drive, keep asking God to protect her and bring forth his will in her life.

Years ago, God nudged my mother with my younger sister's name during the night. Mom jerked awake, jumped out of bed, and prayed for hours. The next morning, while my sister combed her hair, she noticed one of the beige ticks that carry Rocky Mountain Fever hooked into her scalp. My mother rushed her to the doctor for help just in time. Without the protection of my mother's prayer, my sister might have died.

Years before that, God nudged my grandmother awake to pray for my aunt Blanche. A storm rumbled in the distance as Grandma prayed through the night. The next day, she learned a flash flood had swept down a ravine and washed away the boarding school dorm where my aunt had been sleeping. Unable to swim, thrown out a second story window when the building began swaying, my aunt clung to a floating log for hours as her mother prayed. In the morning, rescuers found her, uninjured, several miles from her school, and debris tangled in her hair. Prayer certainly saved her life.

So if God nudges you with a name, pray. Because you won't know what you are supposed to pray for, start by praying for protection for your child. Ask God to protect your child's body, mind, and spirit. Keep praying until you feel God release you from the burden.

You may never find out why God nudged you with a particular name. Kids want their privacy. They may never tell you what was bothering them. They may not even tell you if something catastrophic nearly happened. That's okay. Pray for them anyway. When God whispers a name, don't ignore it. Even if you aren't really sure it's God talking to you and you think it might be just your imagination, pray anyway. It can't hurt. Prayer is always in order. And your prayer may save your child from danger.

Prayerworry

Okay. I'll admit it. Sometimes I worry about my kids and pass it off as prayer. I did it yesterday.

My husband and I drove to a nearby town to watch Tori, our college-age daughter, play soccer. Halfway through the game she headed a ball into the net. A split second later, a player from the opposing team rammed into the side of Tori's head just above the temple. Tori staggered off the field. The trainer half-carried her down the sidelines.

While the rest of the parents watched the continuing game, I hurried around the perimeter of the field. By the time I reached Tori, a fist-sized knot had swelled over her eyebrow and she couldn't remember what day it was. She clutched at her stomach as waves of nausea swept over her.

Knowing I was powerless to do anything, my heart bumped a scared staccato.

The trainer checked her pupils. I prayed, "Lord, protect her brain. Lord heal her. Lord I know researchers have linked declining brain function to soccer head injuries, don't let that happen to her. Lord help her. Please!"

After half an hour of no improvement in Tori's condition, a cold knot of fear twisted in my stomach. Even though I had begged non-stop for God to help her, he didn't seem to be answering. And I was getting little comfort or assurance from prayer.

Suddenly I realized I was concentrating on the *problem* rather than the *Problem Solver*. I was "prayerworrying." I determined to stop.

So while the trainer held an ice pack to my daughter's injury, I turned my "prayerworry" into an effective "prayer of faith" by working through the Romans 8 worry exterminators (found on the next page) then relaxing into Aaron prayers—in the middle of a sporting event.

Tori fully recovered. But even before I knew she would, God gave me peace . . . right there on the soccer field.

Romans 8 Worry Exterminators

Whenever fear and worry over my children threaten me, I practice the following prayer principles:

- **I concentrate on God.**

  "If the Holy Spirit controls your mind, there is life and peace" (Rom. 8:6).

  I force my mind off problems concerning my children and let my thoughts rise to the throne room in heaven where the four living beings continually worship the Father singing, "Holy, holy, holy . . . " I bow in his presence, listening to the thunder rumble, watching the lightning flash from his throne, letting it remind me he has the power to do whatever he pleases.

  I relax and envision Jesus sitting at God's right hand, praying for my children.

- **I ask God to take my fear.**

  "So you should not be like cowering, fearful slaves" (Rom. 8:15).

  Even though I know fear comes from Satan, some twisted part of me wants to grasp it tightly. Maybe I believe fear protects me by helping me prepare for the worst.

That's false. Fear drags my emotions through terrors I may never have to face. Fear multiplies pain. Instead of simply dealing with a problem once, fear tortures me with the same problem over and over.

- **I affirm my children belong to him.**
  "For his Holy Spirit speaks to us deep in our hearts and tells us that we are God's children" (Rom. 8:16).

  I remember that my children really belong to him—not me. He only lent them to me for a few years. No matter how desperately I love them, he loves them more. I thank him for sharing them with me.

- **I give him permission to work his will.**
  "And the Holy Spirit helps us in our distress. For we don't even know what we should pray for nor how we should pray. But the Holy Spirit prays for us . . ." (Rom. 8:26).

  Because the Holy Spirit knows my children better than I do, he knows what is best for them. I may not. So I give him permission to pray for them as he chooses—I ask him to pray God's will into their lives with "groanings" I couldn't comprehend.

- **I trust him to do what's best.**
  "And we know that God causes everything to work together for the good of those who love God and are called according to his purpose for them" (Rom. 8:28).

  I affirm that God is in control. He has a plan for each of my children. He knows everything he intends to do for them. I don't. I determine to trust that he is bringing about the very best for them—no matter how it appears to me. He is continually working in their lives.

- **I believe he loves my children, no matter how things look.**
  "Does it mean he no longer loves us if we have trouble, or are persecuted, or are hungry or cold or in danger or threatened with death? No" (Rom. 8:35–37).

  I realize following the Lord does not render us immune to problems. God never promised us that. As a matter of fact, God often uses difficulties to refine and perfect us. I remind myself that my children will grow stronger through pain and suffering.

- **I proclaim that he is the God of victory.**
  "Despite all these things, overwhelming victory is ours through Christ who loved us" (Rom. 8:37).

  I know he is the God of victory and he generously shares his victory with my children. He is able to bring them through any problem or temptation. They will be successful because he helps them, stays with them, never leaves them. Because he loves them.

  Praise the Lord!

Oops! Wrong Answer

I bumped into Amy at the mall this morning. We hadn't talked since our oldest sons attended preschool together, though two years earlier I had seen her picture in the paper under the caption "Breast Cancer Survivors." We hugged, then chatted over vanilla lattes for an hour before she mentioned her cancer.

"That's the one thing I always prayed I'd never get. I begged God to keep me from breast cancer." Her voice held an incredulous tone. I understood it. We don't expect God, who can spare us if he wants to, to wham us with the very thing we fear most.

"I remember," I said. "You were terrified of it."

Amy nodded. "I was. I was afraid I'd die before I finished raising my kids." She moved her latte cup to the side and leaned forward. "The strange thing is, it was terrible, but God helped me through it. And it drew me so much closer to the Lord, I know I'm a better mother because of it. I'm not sorry it happened." She flashed an impish grin. "God sent a wrong answer to my prayer, and I think it matured me!"

I laughed. As we went our separate ways, I thought about a time recently when God allowed another friend to experience a "wrong answer" to prayer.

Gayle's children played soccer, basketball, and football. Dangerous sports. The one thing she always prayed for them was, "God, protect them from head injury." She begged for that nearly every time she prayed. Yet her son Darren got a concussion in a soccer game on a Wednesday night, then played again the following Saturday morning. That game resulted in two additional head injuries! One on the cheekbone just below the concussion impact, the other on the opposite side of the face. Three head injuries in four days! Two roaring shiners decorated his face. Nausea coiled around in his stomach—a dangerous symptom. Like Amy, Gayle had to accept the very thing she had prayed so desperately against—the very thing she feared most.

Her story ended happily—Darren recovered. And dealing with his head injuries taught her to turn her fears over to God and accept whatever he has for her family. Gayle now understands her children are in God's hands and he will always do what's best for them—*no matter how it looks.*

Do you nurse fears about yourself or your children? Release them. God never actually gives a "wrong answer." Even when we *think* his answers are wrong, they're always right. Trust him to do what's best.

The Wrestling Match

Why don't I pray more? I know prayer works miracles. I *know* my prayers somehow release God's power into the lives of my children. I *know* God will protect them, help them, and bless them when I pray. So what holds me back? Why do I struggle to make myself pray? And when I finally do bow my heart and head to pray for them, why does my mind wander?

I close my eyes and ask the Lord to comfort Ty because he got passed over for the baseball team, and the next thing I know, I've spent the last five minutes stewing because the coach favored his own child over mine! I'm feeling angry right in the middle of prayer! How can that happen? What's wrong with me? I have to take time out to ask God to forgive my anger. Then I feel obligated to pray for the coach, because Jesus instructed us to pray for our enemies. Finally my prayer winds back to Ty.

This is just a guess, but I'll bet the same thing happens to you. There are probably times you are so busy you think you can't possibly pray. And you put it off for days. Then when you finally get around to praying, your mind wanders and you can't concentrate. After a few minutes of alternating between praying *a little* and letting your mind wander *a lot*, you wonder if you've even prayed. Other times you fight drowsiness when you try to pray, and sometimes you actually drift off to sleep.

Do you know why that happens?

Because Satan wants our children, and he doesn't want us to pray. He hates prayer because it keeps him away from them. Prayer thwarts all his evil plans for them. Prayer holds him in check.

So he fights it.

When you don't have time to pray, when your thoughts wander during prayer, when you feel drowsy—you are in a wrestling match with Satan. He can't physically pin you, but he'll try anything and everything to beat you mentally and spiritually. You are fighting him for the very souls of your children.

Don't let him win!

The apostle Paul talks about "wrestling in prayer." Then later, he tells us exactly who we wrestle against. "For we are not fighting against people made of flesh and blood, but against the evil rulers and authorities of the unseen world, against those mighty powers of darkness who rule this world, and against wicked spirits in the heavenly realms" (Eph. 6:12).

When you pray, you aren't alone—even if you are alone. God is listening. And Satan is too. Though he *hates* it.

The instant you focus your thoughts on God, Satan jumps up and down, distracting you, waving worries in front of you. Or, if you're the sort of person who automatically runs to God with worries, Satan will sidetrack you with memories of the sweet card your daughter made for you the night before. He'll do whatever he can do to wrestle your thoughts from God. He intends to beat you.

Don't let him. Don't let him interfere in your relationship with your heavenly Father. Don't let him have your children. Win the match against him the same way you might win a physical wrestling match. *Resist!* You've seen wrestlers strain red-faced against an opponent, muscles bulging. In the same way, you have to strain against Satan with your spirit and mind.

When prayer time rolls around and you are busy—understand the reticence to pray comes from Satan. *Resist* him by forcing yourself to stop your busyness. Pray, even if you aren't in the mood.

Every time Satan pulls your thoughts away from prayer, *resist!* Pull them back to God. Over and over. When Satan drags your thoughts away, *resist!* Yank them back and deliberately concentrate on God again. If your mind wanders fifty times in five minutes, that's okay. Just keep fighting. Reclaim your thoughts every time. Turn them back to prayer the instant you realize your mind has wandered.

If you have to pray out loud to keep awake and focused, do it. If you have to open your eyes and walk around, do it. Write out your prayers. Sing them. Shout them. Do whatever you have to do. Just don't give up. Continue to pull those thoughts back to God. Take every thought captive. Keep praying. *Resist* your enemy. Eventually, he will run off defeated, and you can pray unhindered. Your children will benefit.

Pray for Specific Answers

*K*atrina was barely two the hot summer day she toddled from the house and wandered out of the neighborhood in nothing but a diaper.

Alone.

Easy prey.

By the time her mother, Anna, noticed her empty bed, the baby seemed to have disappeared completely. Anna ran around the house screaming for her.

No answer.

"Heavenly Father," Anna prayed desperately, "help me find her. Set a hedge of protection around her."

She jumped in her car and drove the neighborhood, calling for her child, all the while praying, "Place a hedge of protection around her."

Still there was no sign of Katrina.

For hours Anna searched. Her husband and the neighbors searched. The police were called in. All the while Anna prayed for that hedge of protection.

Near evening the police found Katrina wandering down the sidewalk of a busy street. Several teenagers had formed a circle around her and were guiding her, keeping her from stepping into traffic, guaranteeing no one would molest her.

"We knew she shouldn't talk to strangers," they told the police, "so we tried not to bother her. We just formed kind of a hedge around her to protect her. We knew someone would come looking for her eventually."

God answered Anna's prayer exactly the way she prayed it.

Try praying specifically for your children. It makes the answers really easy to spot.

Pray Against Youthful Sins

*I*f you know your Bible at all, my next statement will shock your socks off: *Job sinned as a youth!* Job! Do you know who he was? Only the most righteous man in the entire Old Testament.

The first verse in the book of Job calls him "blameless." He was so good God sicced Satan onto him: "Have you noticed my servant Job? He is the finest man in all the earth—a man of complete integrity. He fears God and will have nothing to do with evil" (Job 1:8). God had so much confidence in Job's righteousness that he tricked Satan into testing him. And despite all the horrors Satan flung at him, Job refused to sin.

In chapter thirteen, when Job worries that God is remembering the sins of his youth, we realize he wasn't always so blameless. We're never told what he did wrong, just that he sinned back when he was an immature young man.

Like lots of kids do.

Billy Graham's son Franklyn was wayward for several years. His parents prayed for him until his heart softened toward the Lord. Now he is a giant of a man, serving the Lord as he continues his father's ministry, and offering the invocation at President George W. Bush's inauguration.

St. Augustine, a great man of God who lived in the Middle Ages, caroused and womanized in his youth while his mother prayed. For years. Until he finally turned to the Lord.

We aren't told if *Job* had a praying mother, but *your* children do.

Are they rebellious and getting into trouble with the law? Or simply treating you disrespectfully at home? Are they refusing to do homework? Did a teacher catch them cheating on a test? Are they "shacking up"? Have you caught them with pornographic magazines? Do you suspect they lie? Do they refuse to go to church? Do they take drugs?

No matter how big or small their sins may be, don't be discouraged. There is always hope with God. Pray against their "youthful sins." Remember how drastically God changed St. Augustine and Job.

Pray for him to change your children and forgive the sins of their youth.

He will.

Am I Praying Yet?

*I*f your children were to ask you what prayer is, could you tell them? Prayer is more than asking God for favors. It's broader than you might think.

Here's a test for you. If prayer, put a check in the box:

- ☐ Meditating on the Lord
- ☐ Waiting on the Lord; saying nothing; listening
- ☐ Dancing around and shouting "Alleluia" to the Lord
- ☐ Saying, "Praise you, Lord"
- ☐ Thinking about his name and how wonderful it is
- ☐ Begging God to save your husband
- ☐ Petitioning God to protect your children
- ☐ Asking God to heal your friend's cancer
- ☐ Shooting an arrow of thanks heavenward when you barely miss hitting a car

- [ ] Just sitting in his arms; feeling him; saying nothing
- [ ] Singing worship songs, your thoughts focused on him
- [ ] Practicing his presence as you clean toilets
- [ ] Telling God how excited you are about your new job
- [ ] Letting God know you need a new car
- [ ] Prayerfully reading the words of a prayer written a century ago
- [ ] Agreeing with a friend who is offering requests to God
- [ ] Talking to God with your eyes open
- [ ] Speaking to God as you walk or jog
- [ ] Kneeling at a chair crying because you feel his presence so powerfully
- [ ] Listening and assenting as your pastor prays aloud in church
- [ ] Separating off one part of your mind to ask him for help as you talk to someone
- [ ] Lifting your hands and heart to the Lord in worship
- [ ] Lying face down on the floor in grief, yearning for his comfort
- [ ] Pacing as you plead with him
- [ ] Thinking about him as you hang upside down on a roller coaster

If you checked every box, you know what to tell your kids—there are lots of ways to pray. They can pray in any position and they don't have to speak, or even think, words.

But talking to friends about him doesn't count—even though it gives God pleasure. And just thinking and hoping doesn't count. All that counts are the times we turn our spirits to the one true God.

Prayer is all about a relationship with God. Prayer must always be focused on him. And if your children spend enough time doing it, he'll be their friend.

A Pattern for Persistent Prayer
(A retelling of Matthew 15:22–28)

*L*ove for her child led one mother in the New Testament to commit a politically incorrect faux pas. She wasn't supposed to approach Jesus. It wasn't proper. But she did it anyway.

"My daughter has a demon in her and it severely torments her," she told Jesus.

Jesus didn't say a word. He gazed off into the distance.

She didn't get discouraged. She kept pleading for help. She wouldn't quit. Not even when the disciples pushed in and told Jesus to get rid of her. "Her begging is really bugging us," they said. "Tell her to leave."

She wouldn't budge. She kept her eyes fixed on Jesus, *expecting* him to help her. She knew he was good. She just needed to keep asking.

Finally, Jesus met her eyes. "I can't help you. You're a Gentile, and I'm only supposed to help the Jews."

She saw the compassion in his eyes, heard the sorrow in his voice, and her heart swelled with love and admiration. Throwing herself at his feet, she worshipped him. For a while, all thoughts of her daughter vanished and she thought only about the sweetness of the Lord.

Then the memory of her daughter's pain floated back. She looked up, tears streaming down her face and pled with Jesus again. "Please, help me."

"It wouldn't be right," Jesus said. "I can't take food from the children and throw it to the dogs." But the resolve had left his voice.

"I know you're right," her voice was barely more than a whisper, "but even dogs are allowed to lick up crumbs when they fall under their master's table." She dropped her eyes, waiting for his answer.

"You have great faith." He sighed and shook his head. "I'll do it. Your daughter is healed."

Zap! That was it. Her daughter was healed instantly. Persistent prayer paid off.

But there was a pattern to the mother's actions. She didn't just plead "gimme, gimme, gimme" or "please, please, please" over and over—which is how we tend to view persistent prayer. Her prayer to Jesus contained three elements:

1. *She had faith.* She kept praying for Jesus' help because she knew who he was and she knew he would help her eventually, even though she didn't deserve it.
2. *She stopped to worship* right in the middle of her plea for help. Even before Jesus said yes, she revered him, appreciated him, adored him.
3. *She refused to stop asking.* Nothing could dissuade her. Not the disciples's rudeness, not Jesus' apparent refusal. She knew he wouldn't want her daughter to suffer from demon possession. She knew he could help her if he chose to.

Jesus is just as capable of answering prayers today as he was then.

So don't give up praying for your child. Ask every day. Plead with God many times a day.

God is powerful. He can do more than you can imagine. He can save your child, heal your child, protect your child. Believe in him.

And remember to worship and praise him in the midst of your asking.

I Don't Want to Bother God

"You're a good girl, Pearl," her mama always said. And it was true. Pearl loved her parents and she loved the Lord, but she never asked him for anything. She didn't even ask him to ease her pain when she broke her ribs because, she said, "I shouldn't bother him. He has lots more important things to think about." Besides, her mother took her to the doctor and her ribs healed just fine.

Pearl thought if she could get through problems without bothering God, she should. She thought she was being considerate of God. She wasn't. She didn't understand our Father.

He's our Daddy. It thrills him to meet our needs.

Just as it thrilled me to help my oldest son a few years ago.

I sat alone on the couch reading a book, feeling depressed. It was my sixteenth wedding anniversary. My husband had been out of town for over a week and I missed him. The three children slept downstairs in their bedrooms. The clock showed nearly midnight.

"Mom?" My fourteen-year-old son's faint voice came from the stairway.

My head shot up. "Ty?" I closed my book and laid it on the end table.

Ty appeared at the top of the stairs looking flushed. Groaning, he lowered himself to the floor and lay flat, with his cheek and bare arms pressed against the cool ceramic tiles. He used to do this whenever he had a temperature. He hadn't done it in years. "I feel terrible."

I rushed over to feel his face with the back of my hand. Burning hot. "You have a temperature, Honey."

He groaned again. I sat beside him rubbing his back—something he wouldn't let me do lately. He was too grown up.

"Why don't you come sleep in my bed so I can keep an eye on you?" I expected him to say no. He hadn't jumped in bed with my husband and me since he was a toddler. He didn't even like being hugged anymore. I missed it.

"Okay," he moaned. I helped him into my queen-sized bed and went to grab the thermometer.

Through the rest of the night I stayed awake, feeding him water from a teaspoon, mopping his face and arms with a damp washcloth, checking his temperature, and cleaning up when he vomited. By morning he felt better and I was exhausted.

But content.

I loved mothering Ty again. Though I didn't want him to be sick, it made me feel wonderful to be able to help him. And I loved it that he came to me when he needed help. It would have made me feel terrible if he had lain downstairs in his bedroom, sick and suffering, and not called for me because he worried he might bother me.

I think you get it, don't you? Our Daddy God *wants* us to bother him. He loves helping us—just as I loved helping Ty. Just as you love helping your children.

Doesn't it touch our hearts when our little ones look up to us, big eyes brimming with tears? We want to help them when their little bodies hurt, when other children taunt them.

Just as they touch our hearts, we touch God's heart.

Our Daddy loves us. How terrible it must be for him to look down and watch us suffering on this planet that his enemy has invaded and damaged. How awful for him to have to watch the enemy torture his beloved children.

Isaiah 63:9 says that in all our suffering God suffers with us. Just as we hurt with our children when they hurt. He longs for us to call out to him. He wants to ease our pain. But he can't do it unless we ask him to.

Pearl wouldn't ask for God's help because she yearned to be nice to him. How sad. She didn't understand how very much he longed for her to bother him—so he could be her Daddy and help her.

God loves you. If you have a need—if your children have needs—hold up your arms to him like a toddler who needs her mother. Don't waste your whole life trying to handle small problems alone. Ask God for help. And make certain your children know how often you do it. Tell them God smiles with delight every time they "bother" him.

God Wants Us to Ask

I can't think of a single place in the Bible where someone asked God for help and he said, "Are you kidding? Again? Don't I ever get a break?"

The closest he comes is in Exodus 14:15 when he says to Moses, "Why are you crying out to me? Tell the people to get moving!" But he isn't saying, don't ask. He's saying, hellooo. I already answered. Let's get the show on the road.

Many places in the Bible feel like God is *begging* us to pray to him.

- He urges Jeremiah, "Call to me, and I will answer you, and show you great and mighty things, which you do not know" (Jer. 33:3 NIV).
- When Jesus knows he has only a few hours left with his disciples, he pleads over and over for them not to forget to ask him for the things they want. "Yes, ask anything in my name, and I will do it" (John 14:14). Read chapters fourteen through sixteen in John's gospel. You'll be amazed at all the times he urges them to ask.

- Jesus' brother reprimands believers in the early church for not asking: "The reason you don't have what you want is that you don't ask God for it" (James 4:2).

Nothing has changed. He still wants us to ask. The words in the Bible are meant for you.

He longs for you to ask in prayer. He longs for your children to ask in prayer. But he can't help if you don't ask—if they don't ask.

Burn that truth into your children's brains. Help them develop the habit of *asking* God. When they're afraid, say, "Let's pray together about it, Sweetheart. God wants us to *ask* for his help." When they need help with a test, remind them to *ask* God to help them study and refresh their minds as they take it. *Ask* with them for God to send the right life mate.

A popular radio talk-show host claims that once you hear something thirteen times it becomes truth. Tell them more than thirteen times. Stress *asking*, the same way God told the Israelites to pass on the law to their children: "Repeat them again and again to your children. Talk about them at home and when you are away on a journey, when you are lying down and when you are getting up. Tie them to your hands as a reminder. And wear them on your forehead. Write them on the door posts of your house and on your gates" (Deut. 6:7–9).

Don't ever stop reminding your children to *ask* God in prayer for anything . . . everything. Nag them to *ask, ask, ask.* Then bow your head and *ask* God to shape your children into men and women of prayer.

Know the Rules

I have the world's best pastor, Ron Mehl. A godly spirit radiates from him when he stands to preach. I hang on his every word. I completely trust his interpretations of the Bible and his child-rearing advice. But you know what? Not even Ron Mehl can give me a complete picture of how God wants my children to look on the inside.

Only God can do that. And the only place to find out what God says is in the Bible. So if you want to do the best job possible for your children, if you want to know exactly how to train them and how to pray for right traits and attitudes, you have to read the Bible.

Every day.

Twenty-five years ago, God used a difficult time in my life to catapult me into daily Bible reading. I was raised in a parsonage and attended Christian college, but I never read the Bible until I encountered a relationship I had no idea how to handle. Though normally an upbeat person, I sank into a deep depression, crying for hours at a time. I couldn't talk to anyone about the problem. I kept thinking, "If I just knew what to do, I'd do it."

After months of unhappiness, I turned to the Bible as a last resort. To my amazement, I found comfort and answers in its pages. So much so that—and I kind of hate to admit this because I know so many people find it difficult to read the Bible—I *loved* it. Once I read for eight hours straight.

When the babies came and it got more difficult to find time to read, I made a rule. I didn't *have* to open my Bible if I didn't want to, but I wasn't allowed any "me" time until I had read it. No sewing, no television, no chatting on the phone. The Bible came first.

It told me everything I needed for child rearing. I color-coded verses to pray for my children: blue for lies, red for anger, green for discipline, pink for love, yellow for verses about friends. Then I'd pray a red verse when I saw an anger problem in my children, a blue verse when one of them lied. I set verses to music, and we sang them on the way to baseball practice. When my children fought, I made them quote, "It is to a man's honor to avoid strife, but every fool is quick to quarrel" (Prov. 20:3 NIV). Then I prayed for them not to fight.

I still love reading the Bible. Every time I open it I find some gift to request for my children. I want their characters rich with righteousness.

If you want your children to maximize their potential, you need to read it, too. Then you can pray its principles into your children. Here are a few suggestions to help establish a habit of regular reading:

I. **Buy one of the new readable versions.** They are as accurate as the *King James,* but their language is modern—easy to understand. My favorite right now is the *New Living Translation.* However, I also enjoy the *New International Version*, and the *New King James*. You may find another you prefer.

2. **Ask the Lord to give you a strong desire to read his Word.** He chooses us, we don't choose him. Unless he puts the desire in your heart to read his Word, you won't want to. If you feel your heart burning within you to read right now—thank him. The desire is a gift from him.

3. **Ask the Holy Spirit to guide you as you read.** Without his help, we can't understand even the modern versions. God's words are spiritually discerned, so every day before I begin reading, I ask the Holy Spirit to give me the gift of understanding, to help me understand as I read, to lift the veil from my eyes and let me see something I've never noticed or understood before.

4. **Set a goal.** Determine to read daily. Ask God to show you how much you should tackle each day. Be easy on yourself. If a chapter is all you can manage, that's fine. My goal is three chapters per day, six days a week. I allow myself Sundays off because I'll be worshiping at church.

5. **Don't allow yourself any "me" time until you've read.** Guard your time in the word. Make sure you read before you do anything for yourself. You'll begin to love it so much you won't want to miss a day.

6. **Claim God's promises for yourself and your children.** Claim promises for your children by inserting their names into verses. Read: "Now (child's name) has every spiritual gift (child's name) needs. . . . He will keep (child's name) strong right up to the end, and he will keep (child's name) free from all blame on the great

day when our Lord Jesus Christ returns. God will surely do this for (my child's name) for he always does just what he says . . . " (I Cor. I:7–9).

The Bible can help you understand what your children need to make them successful and happy. It's time to get started. Read the scriptures. Pray them into your children.

How I Pray for My Children

I didn't take to motherhood naturally. My son's aunt Joan gave him his first bath because I feared I couldn't do it right. Still, within a very few days I became a pro at tending to his physical needs. I rocked him, fed him, changed his diaper, kissed his little feet, danced around the living room giggling with him. I loved it.

However, instilling godly values was a different story. I was not a person of wisdom, and I knew it. I lacked even common sense. I understood early on that I needed to hunt out child-rearing principles from the Bible and also to *pray over everything*. If I didn't, I'd have a disaster on my hands.

I needed help with everything—and the Lord graciously gave it to me.

When Ty's nose ran or his tummy hurt, I prayed. When he insisted on ripping all the books off the shelves, when my six-month-old second child howled in anger at her brother, when the boys broke Tori's front tooth in a pillow fight, I prayed and disciplined them. When Tevin snapped his tibia in half, I prayed all the way to the hospital.

I diligently studied my children, watching for anything that might call for prayer.

Shortly after their births, I started on the most important prayer of all. "Dear Jesus, please save my children's souls. Make them *want* to follow you." By age five, each had responded by accepting Jesus as their personal Savior. What a thrill for a mother!

After that, I settled into the regular pattern of prayer I still follow. I pray for specific godly character traits for each of them. I ask God to make them loving and kind to others, keep them from laziness, give them godly friends, prepare the right spouse for them. When they tell me of loneliness, trouble with friends, injury, or illness, I spend extra time praying.

Every morning, I pray an umbrella of protection over them. I ask God to protect their minds, spirits, hearts, attitudes, and bodies. I remind him that the most important thing is for them to keep their hearts right. I ask him to preserve and increase the relationship they have with him. I breathe prayers for their righteousness off and on all day long.

Recently, the Lord convicted me for keeping my prayers too *defensive*. He told me to pray *aggressively*. So I started praying more for my children to shine as lights and examples to the people around them. Within a week, Ty called from grad school asking me to send a book for a fellow student who is mad at God. And since then, all three have mentioned chats with friends who don't know the Lord.

Though I can't observe them as closely now that they are all away at school, I am confident the Lord will keep directing my prayers for them. Praying for them is the most important job I've ever held—a lifelong job. I will pray for them as long as I have breath.

A Date with God

*S*ue told me about a date with her daughter Mallory. They sat side by side in vinyl salon chairs while two manicurists pampered them. "It was wonderful," Sue said. "Mallory loved it because she'd never had her nails done before. But for me, the best part was being alone together. We rarely take time for that. It brought us so much closer. "

Do you think your Abba Father longs to spend time alone with you? If you haven't already set aside a daily date time when you can be by yourself with him, I hope you will. You need time alone to develop relationship. It can be anywhere, anytime. It just needs to be your regular time with the one who loves you, in a quiet place where you can talk over your concerns with him, where you can whisper how you enjoyed your baby's first steps or the letter from your married daughter.

Set a minimum amount of time for your daily date. Give up one thirty-minute television show and spend the time with God. Or if that is too long, start with five minutes. A little time is better than no time.

Once you've established a pattern, tell your children about your date time and invite them on a group date with you and God. Maybe you could simply pray a little longer with them at bedtime for a date or sit in the car before a soccer practice. But make it formal. Tell them the purpose is to get to know God better.

My daughter initiated my favorite group date with God. In high school, she regularly switched off all the lights in our bonus room and played Christian music on the stereo. She'd relax in a blue swivel recliner while she worshiped the Lord. Because it was her time with God, I tried not to interrupt, but I loved to pull up a matching rocking chair and worship with her. We often passed as much as two hours that way. Then sometimes she would begin to talk quietly to me—about friends, her day, the Lord. In the midst of growing closer to God, the relationship between my daughter and me grew stronger, too.

Those are precious memories. You can't force something like that to happen with your children. But be assured, just as you grow close to your children when you spend time with them, you will grow close to God if you'll spend time with him. He promises. And he's waiting. It's up to you. "Draw close to God, and God will draw close to you" (James 4:7).

Ceaseless Prayer

I've read lots of books on prayer, and I think all of them dealt with the subject of ceaseless prayer. They pretty much *had* to because Paul commands us to "Pray without ceasing" (1 Thess. 4:17 NKJV). But each book I read came up with a different idea about what Paul meant.

One book said Paul meant we are to have an attitude of prayer throughout the day. Another suggested we simply need to remember to turn to God immediately whenever we need help. My favorite said the Holy Spirit within us prays constantly for our concerns, and we don't have to do much of anything for ceaseless prayer to happen. They all agreed we couldn't possibly think every thought about God.

I *want* to pray without ceasing. I try. But frankly, I don't know if I do or not. And I don't think I'll know for sure until Jesus reveals everything to me in heaven. But the way the New Living Translation renders the verse on ceaseless prayer encourages me. It simply says, "Keep on praying." Never give up. Pray whenever you think about it. Keep trying.

That's how I pray for my children. Nearly every time they flit across my mind I breathe a brief prayer for them. "Lord work your will in their lives," or "Keep their hearts tender," or "Set their hearts on fire for you." One of my favorites is, "Grant them spiritual maturity beyond their years."

I pray in my car, when I do housework, and at sporting events. Because my prayer partner and my walking partner are one and the same, when we walk we pray conversationally for our children.

And any time something good happens, I thank the Lord for it—out loud if possible.

Is that ceaseless prayer? I don't know. I spend a lot of time thinking thoughts that aren't prayer, saying words that aren't prayer. I'm not worried about it. God understands. As long as I keep on trying to pray ceaselessly, I think he is pleased.

Prayer for Future Spouses

*I*t's never too early to start praying for the future spouses of your children. Their future mates are out there somewhere. Right now. You don't know their names or see their faces, but God does. As you pray for your son's wife or your daughter's husband, God knows exactly who that person is. He will answer your prayers for them, just as he answers prayers for your own children. By praying for them now, you can help open the way for God and their parents to shape them into godly people who match your own children. Your prayers *now* will have a lot to do with the quality of life your children experience for their entire married life. And though they may spend eighteen years with you, they will spend fifty with their mates.

If you don't want your son married to a woman who nags him to distraction and continually criticizes him, pray a gentle, kind spirit into his future wife. If you don't want your daughter married to a workaholic who puts his own interests ahead of her and the children, pray for him to develop correct priorities as he matures—no matter what he sees in his own parents.

Ask God to give the parents of these children wisdom as they discipline. Ask God to make the marriages of the parents strong so that these children have a good model to follow.

Pray for the Lord to protect their future mates from obvious evils like drugs, pornography, and sexual abuse. Pray for the same character traits you pray into your own children.

Plead with God to show himself to your future children and lead them into a deep relationship with him. Ask him to help them understand marriage as a partnership for the purpose of spiritual growth. Ask that the relationships they will develop with your children always hold him at the center.

Pray for purity for your children as well as each of their future mates. Plead with him to help them all *determine* to refrain from sex until marriage. Pray that, once married, they succeed in keeping all sexual intimacy inside marriage. Pray for them to stay faithful, even in their thoughts.

Ask God to give them proper expectations for marriage. Help them realize that the initial spark will fade, but that is the time to develop stronger love.

If you haven't started praying for your children's future mates, it's time. I started when my children were small. I've heard of moms who started praying for future mates when they first realized they were pregnant. But it's never too late, even if your children are already married.

Phone Prayers

I think it started with my friend Helen. We're both writers, so our phone conversations often begin with talk about books. But it rarely takes long for our chats to drift to our children. As soon as a need is mentioned, Helen always says, "Well, let's pray about that right now." So I close my eyes while she prays, then at the first lull, I lift my voice to the Lord. It's wonderful.

But phone prayers with Helen are long distance.

Cherie lives forty-five minutes across town. Too far away to meet in person very often, but the call is free. We used to keep in touch via phone; now we spend the majority of our time on the phone praying. When one of us calls the other, we spend a minute or two on initial greetings, then we launch into prayer—first for our own children, then for the children of our friends and relatives. If one of us has news or needs, the other hears about them as we take them to the Lord in thanks or as requests.

We both love praying for our children that way, but I've gained an added benefit. I tend to be a complainer. I love venting my problems to friends, and I'm not sure it's wrong since the Bible says to bear one another's burdens. But when Cherie and I pray to the Lord rather than just talking to each other, the temptation to complain is erased. I feel supported and encouraged by her *and* the Lord. Plus, he can actually solve my problems. Phone prayers are a win/win situation.

Is It Okay to Pray for Things I Don't Really Need?

What do you need? What do your children need? Really need? Think about it for a second before you continue reading.

I heard recently about a man in a famine-starved country in Africa. The man had hoped his family could survive at home—until his oldest son died of starvation. Without taking time to grieve properly, the man took his wife and two young children and started on the three-day walk to the feeding station. A day into the trip, his wife and children collapsed at the side of the road, unable to walk further.

The man summoned all his strength and picked up a child in each arm. He struggled on down the road toward the feeding station, continually turning around to make sure he could still see his wife. Just before she disappeared from view, he lowered his precious children to the ground and turned to walk back the way he had just come. Lifting his wife in his arms, he trudged up the road to where his children lay. When he reached them, he settled her onto the ground, hoisted them into his arms and continued the next quarter mile.

He kept this up for two more days, until finally he arrived at the feeding station where he gratefully accepted food and shelter for his family. Their needs met, they all survived.

Okay, now tell me. What do you and your children really need? Probably not much. I know my family doesn't. We live in a nation blessed by God. Our physical needs are few.

But our children have tremendous spiritual needs, even if they are Christians. The blessings we enjoy do little to develop their character. The images flickering from television and movie screens draw them toward unspeakable evil. Drug-and-alcohol-addicted peers stagger around them. The violence in our society tempts them to fear. Satan fights for their souls every day of their lives.

Your children *need* the Lord. They *need* his guidance and protection. They *need* his Holy Spirit to fill them. They *need* contented godly attitudes. They *need* to understand how much he loves them.

I don't think God minds if you ask him for a new family computer for Christmas, a nicer car, expensive coats for every member of the family, or even to win a contest. He wants you to ask for things, and he just might grant every single request. "Take delight in the Lord, and he will give you your heart's desires" (Ps. 37:4). So delight in him, enjoy him, and make him your first priority. Then go ahead and ask—for anything.

Just remember the real *needs* of your children. Don't forget to pray for them, too.

Should I Fast for My Children?

*M*y friend Emily lived next door to a woman who was not a believer. Emily longed to talk to her about the Lord, but shyness held her back—for five years. One day Emily decided to fast for ten days. She drank juices and water as she prayed, but ate no food. She prayed a little for her neighbor, but focused most of her prayers on her children and unsaved sister. Nevertheless, on the seventh day of her fast, the neighbor knocked on her door and asked Emily to tell her about Jesus! Somehow, Emily's prayer had unlocked power that allowed the Lord to work in her neighbor's heart.

When teaching about fasting, Jesus said, "And your Father, who knows all secrets, will reward you" (Matt. 6:18). I think Jesus meant not only that God would reward us in heaven for fasting, but also he would reward us with answers to prayer now.

Emily prayed for her neighbor for five years. God rewarded her with a yes answer when she fasted. The fasting seemed to release extra power in the spiritual realm.

Jesus spoke of the power of fasting when his disciples tried unsuccessfully to cast out some demons. They had been able to cast them out before, so when they couldn't do it that time, they asked him why. He said, "This kind does not go out except by prayer and fasting" (Matt. 17:21 NKJV). Prayer and fasting together seem to unlock the key to the impossible.

Not all prayers for your children require going without food. But if one of your children is having a particularly difficult time and you aren't seeing your prayers answered, you might try fasting. Somehow it pulls extra strength into your prayers.

No One Else Will Do It

We work so hard to give our children every advantage. We buy nice clothes. Check out the schools for excellence. Pay big bucks for them to play on the right sports teams and even bigger bucks for the right college.

We do our best to protect them. We make them wear seat belts and warm coats. Locks on our doors and windows keep them safe at night. When they choose wrong friends, we help them reevaluate and understand their choices.

All those things are wonderful—a mark of good parenting. But I wonder if we realize how much more prayer can do than any of those things. Prayer will lead your children to Christ and give them eternal life! Prayer will do more to guarantee your children success and happiness than anything else on the face of the earth . . . because it isn't limited to earth. It reaches up to heaven to the one who weaves all experiences for good. With him, it reaches inside your children's minds and hearts and guides them toward glorious futures.

You don't have to live near them. Distance means nothing to prayer. It reaches across the miles. If someone else has custody of your children, you can still love them and influence them through prayer. If a child has rebelled and turned from you or run away from home and you have no idea where to find him, you can still have a part in their lives through prayer. You can offer them actual help in trouble even though you can't see or touch them. God will nudge you to caress them with prayer when they need it.

Praying for your children is your responsibility. Your blessing. No one will ever pray for your child as often or with the intensity you do. No one. Because no one loves your children as much as you do, and love adds fervency and frequency to prayers.

Prayer is the greatest advantage you can offer your children. The greatest treasure anyone can give them. You don't have to be wealthy to pray. Prayer is free. You don't need lots of leisure time to do it. You can pray while you work.

Prayers change lives. Especially when the one praying is a mom.

The Responsibility Never Fades

*E*very morning I call my parents who live across the country. I listen sadly as my mother tells me about my father's physical difficulties. Blind for nearly ten years now and almost deaf, he can no longer read the Bible and the books that were so precious to him in his youth. But it hasn't kept him from his most important task. "I hear him wandering through the house praying out loud lots of times," she confided to me recently. "He's so wrapped up in conversation with the Lord, I'm not sure he knows he's talking out loud."

Dad isn't the only one who prays. Whenever any of my children go through difficulties, Mom is still the first one I tell. She grabs the problem and holds it up before the Lord all day long. I know, because the next morning when I call she often tells me, "I even woke up in the middle of the night praying."

"I could feel your prayers," I tell her. And it's true. The minute she starts to pray, peace envelops me.

My husband's ninety-one-year-old father lies bedridden in a nursing home. When pain keeps him awake at night, he prays for my children. "Did you ever pray for two or three hours at a time?" he once asked me. His voice broke and he looked away. I knew he meant he had spent his night praying, and I felt so fortunate to know him.

Though bodies fade in old age, spirits grow stronger. Grandparents have more time and wisdom to pray for children than they did in their youth. And prayer is by far the most important job they've held. The job never ends.

How blessed you are if you have parents that still pray for you and your children. How blessed your children are if you are a praying grandparent. You *will* bear fruit in old age—just as God promised: "Even in old age they will still produce fruit" (Ps. 92:14).

And the fruit you bear is most precious in God's sight—the fruit of godly children.

Section Two

Ideas for Praying throughout the Day

Ideas for Praying throughout the Day

- Throughout the day, work at turning negative thoughts into positive prayer. Instead of thinking, "If I have to pick up one more dirty sock I'm going to tell *him* to put a sock in it," pray, "Lord, thank you for teaching me patience."
- Practice the presence of Jesus as you do dishes or vacuum the carpet. Visualize him right there with you, delighting in your hard work. Feel his love and approval of you.
- Psalms are prayers. Pick one and pray it.
- Praise the Lord out loud—at the top of your lungs—when you are alone. If you feel brave, praise him aloud when you're *not* alone.
- Instead of napping, turn on worship music and dance your praises to the Lord. Decide which refreshes you more—a nap or the Lord.
- Walk around your yard and house asking the Lord to bless them and use them for his glory.

- Ask God to show you and your family how valuable you all are to him. A hint: Romans 12:3 says we are to measure our value by how much faith he has given us.
- Spend five minutes praying against worthlessness. Pray this for yourself, your children, your husband, and your friends.
- Whenever your child tells you something nice that happened at school, bow your heads together and thank God for this blessing.
- Prayerfully sing worship songs—all day or until your voice gives out.
- Reprogram your computer screensaver so that it runs the verse you are currently praying.
- Throughout the day remember, whatever takes your focus from God is the enemy's stronghold in your life. Ask God to keep you focused on him.
- Give your children "spiritual baths" by bathing them in prayer. Ask God to cleanse them of any impure thoughts or actions. Pray, "Wash them and they'll be clean" (Ps. 51:10).
- For children who no longer live in the home: At the beginning of each week, send the verses you intend to pray that week to them. Each day they will remember how you are praying and be comforted.
- Post the daily verse on your refrigerator so your children can know exactly how you are praying for them and take strength from it as they go about the day.
- Morning, noon, and night, pray for God to release his ministering angels around your children to protect them.

- Praise God that he is the fortress in which you and your family hide. Praise him because he can extinguish the fiery darts Satan shoots at your children.
- Ask God to bless your children beyond anything you can imagine. Say, "Surprise me, Lord."
- Ask God to do whatever is necessary today to keep your children on his path. Give him permission to use any means to change any wrong direction they choose.
- Tuck a brief written prayer into your children's lunch boxes. Remind them they are loved by you and God.
- Tuck a note into your children's lunch boxes or books, promising to pray while they are at school. Mention a specific problem you have spoken about together if it isn't something that would embarrass them.
- Sit in a comfortable chair. Set the timer for five minutes. Ask God to bring each child's characteristics to mind. Thank him for each of them. Ask him to strengthen the good aspect of each trait.
- Ask God to reveal your children's weaknesses to you. Then instead of worrying, pray for God to strengthen those areas of weakness.
- Ask God to use any weakness in your children to humble them and draw them closer to him.
- Ask God to send strong Christians into the lives of your children to encourage and bless them.
- Ask God to make your children examples who will draw the people around them into a closer relationship with the Lord.

- Petition God, in Jesus' name, to help your children learn to fill all their needs with him rather than searching for someone else to fill their needs.
- Pray for a spirit of truth to surround your family like a hedge.
- Thank God that although he *could* make everything in the lives of your children right with one touch, he does it little by little so they will develop a relationship with him by depending on him.
- Ask the Lord to help your children respond to his prompting so they will learn to recognize his voice.
- Praise God that he has prepared good works for your children to do for him. Ask him to fortify them to accomplish those good works.
- Cry to the Lord to arise and fight for your children and defeat their strong enemies. Then praise him—because praise defeats the enemy (see Psalm 8:2).
- Take authority over every nightmare attacking your children in their sleep. Declare victory over them in the strong name of Jesus.
- Praise God because he has blessed your children and will continue to bless them.
- Walk around all day speaking aloud all the good things you know about God. Start with the book of Genesis and continue through to Revelation. Then thank him for personal blessings and miracles.
- Thank God that the name of Jesus and his precious blood protects you and your children.

- Confess your sins to the Lord. Ask him to deal with your children and make them eager to confess and receive forgiveness for every sin they commit.
- Remember that maturity could be defined as knowing right from wrong. Ask God to make you and your children mature.
- Praise God that your children are blessed and highly favored.
- In the name of Jesus, come against the spirit of fear. Ask him to give your children courage to face everything life sends their way.
- *First* thing when you awaken in the morning, pray for your kids. *Last* thing at night, as you drift off to sleep, name them to the Lord.
- Make reading the Bible daily an iron-clad rule in your life. Thank the Lord that it will guide you as you pray for your children.

Section Three

Thirty-One Days of Prayer

No Prayer Giants Allowed

When my friends Bette and Petey pray, I feel the power of the Holy Spirit sweep into the room. I listen entranced. Their eloquent words curl around me, comforting me, encouraging me.

Proving how inadequate I am.

Why can't I pray beautiful words like they do? I love Jesus. But when I try to talk to him, I fumble with the words. Sometimes they tumble out so fast they tie up my tongue. Other times I sit dumbly, overwhelmed by his presence—unable to think of a single word.

I know that is all right with God. He simply desires a right attitude . . . a heart that seeks after him. He doesn't require me to speak impressive words.

But I long to.

Not so someone else can hear. I want to do it for him.

And I've come up with a solution. Because his words are not only beautiful—but alive—I just pray them back to him. I pick a verse from the Bible and speak it to him. I ask him to bless my family with everything the verse promises. I ask him to help my children obediently follow its instruction. I keep my mind on the verse as my prayer branches out.

And suddenly, as I pray God's words back to him, my words sound a little more pleasing—at least to me.

In this section, I've written out some of the scripture-based prayers I speak for my own children. I hope you will pray them each day for your children, too.

Day One
My Children Can Delight God

Great and powerful God,

It amazes me that you created my children to give you pleasure. You! The King of all the kings, the Creator of the universe! Thank you, blessed God, that through love you chose to adopt them as your own children—sons and daughters of the King. Not only do you consider them valuable, but when they act righteously, they actually bring you delight!

Lord, help them to grasp the depth of your love. Help them understand that your great love for them sometimes causes you pain. Because you care for them, you suffer with them when they suffer. You grieve when their hearts harden and they turn away from you. You hate it when greed lures them to exchange loyalty to you for earthly goods and pleasures.

Lead them into attitudes and behaviors that shine delight into your heart. Move them to return your love. Let devotion to you motivate them to place you first and serve you fervently. Help them love you with all their souls, hearts, and minds. Infuse their characters with faithfulness. Mold them into encouragers who touch the lives of anyone who happens near them.

A loving mom,

"For you created everything, and it is for your pleasure they exist and were created."
(Rev. 4:11)

Further prayer suggestions:

- In the space below, write one or two attitudes you know would delight the Lord. Pray for your children to exhibit those attitudes today.
- Pray for God to reveal his love to your children.

Day Two
Forgiveness

Gracious Father,

I praise you for your precious gift of forgiveness. Nothing feels better. Nothing brings such relief! Thank you that the instant my children sin, all they have to do is repent and—Whoosh!—their guilt is gone. Forever. No matter how ugly and filthy their sins were, you make them clean new creatures. Because of Jesus' sacrifice on the cross, you erase their sins from your mind and see them as righteous, just like your Son.

Lord, help my children remember the cross. Help them to turn to you and beg for forgiveness when they sin. Help them to accept your forgiveness. Help them know beyond any doubt that you *always* forgive. Show them that any guilt left over after they have asked you to forgive them is *false* guilt. Please don't let false guilt drag them into depression, keep them from you, or make them feel unworthy.

When feelings of worthlessness overcome them, help them to instantly recognize Satan's fingerprints and remember he is the one who wants them to feel bad. You don't. You simply want them to ask for forgiveness and repent. Teach them not to feel ashamed for sins you've forgiven and forgotten. In Jesus' name I pray, amen.

A mom who has been forgiven,

"If you forgive those who sin against you, your heavenly Father will forgive you." (Matt. 6:14–15)

Further prayer suggestions:

- Pray for your children to recognize false guilt and reject it.
- Ask the Lord to help them replace memories of past sins with thoughts of good things.
- Tell God you know he has the power to call your unsaved children to repentance. Thank God that he *will* call your children to repentance and forgive their sins.

Day Three
Forgiving Others

Dear Father,

I praise you for the life-changing forgiveness you offer to my children. Show them that if they want your forgiveness, they must give up any resentment and bitterness they harbor in their hearts. Help them to hold out to others the forgiveness you have given to them.

When that feels impossible to them, remind them that the first step in forgiveness is simply giving their pain to you, giving up the right to punish the person who hurt them and giving you permission to mete out justice to that person instead. Each time the pain or anger comes to mind, help them to turn heavenward and ask you to help them release their right for revenge one more time—even if the offense springs to mind a thousand times a day. Even if every person they know says they have a right to hold a grudge. Remind them that you said we must forgive seventy times seven if we expect forgiveness from you.

Make them understand that anyone who sins against them sins first against you, so you are suffering right along with them. They are never alone in their pain. Help them to accept your love and forgiveness as they forgive others. In Jesus' name, amen.

A mom who desires loving, forgiving children,

"But if you refuse to forgive others, your Father will not forgive your sins." (Matt. 6:14–15)

Further prayer suggestions:

- Ask the Lord to reveal any unforgiveness in your own heart. Release those feelings of hurt to the Lord.
- Ask him to let you be an example to your children.

Day Four
Attending Church

Gracious Father,

I magnify you for creating my children to belong to the body of Christ. Help my children understand how important it is to attend church and join other believers in honoring you. Help them to think of church as a place where they can feel your presence magnified because you are present in each Christian. Help them to realize they need never be alone—because your spiritual family is their true family.

As they grow older, give them discernment to find a church that studies your Word and focuses on you, a church *alive* with your Spirit, where they can develop and grow and use their gifts. Help them find a church with a spirit of love and unity where the people will gently warn them if they start down a wrong path. Let them enjoy warm fellowship with their church family.

Give my children a strong desire to contribute to the body of believers, to encourage and help out when needed, to lift up other members of the body in prayer, and to speak kind words. If they are tempted to try to live the Christian life without meeting with fellow believers, show them one reason for attending church is to fulfill their responsibility to other Christians. I pray this in your name, Jesus, amen.

A concerned mom,

"And let us not neglect our meeting together, as some people do." (Heb. 10:25)

Further prayer suggestions:

- Pray for wisdom for your young children's Sunday school teachers.
- If your children go to a different church than you do, pray for their church and yours.
- Ask the Lord to help your children really listen to the wisdom offered at church.
- Pray for God to open their hearts to the truth.

Day Five
Good Work Habits

Dear heavenly Father,

I know that you want my children to do the very best they can at whatever they find to do, whether it is homework, chores at home, helping out a neighbor, or a job outside the home. I thank you for gifting each of my children in special ways. I praise you that they possess the ability to serve you through work, even if they have disabilities that keep them from doing what others would usually consider work.

Please remove any laziness that has crept in to cripple my children's good character. Take away the rebellion that tempts them to give in to laziness. Make them diligent, desiring to work hard to please you. Show them how to do their best at anything they take on.

Show me ways to model hard work and instill godly character. Please forgive me for the times I have failed to do so. Forgive me for allowing them to sit too long in front of the television. Forgive me for the times I didn't speak up when they chose to play computer games when homework wasn't done. Forgive me for letting them shirk chores.

In Jesus' name, I ask you to make them hard workers, making the most of their time so they will please you, amen.

A mom who wants her children to work for God,

"Work hard and cheerfully at whatever you do, as though you were working for the Lord rather than for people." (Col. 3:23)

Further prayer suggestions:

- In the space below, list the names of your children along with one spiritual or physical gift for each. Thank God for them as you write.
- Ask the Lord to show you ways to teach them how to work hard.
- Pray that they will put work in the right perspective, not becoming perfectionistic workaholics, but doing their best to please the Lord.

Day Six
My Treasure—God's Treasure

Lord,

I praise you for your great love for my children. I rejoice that you work continuously in their lives, even when I don't see it, even when I feel discouraged over glitches I see in their behavior and attitudes. Thank you that those flaws are even more apparent to you than to me . . . and you have the power to heal them. Thank you for the corrective troubles and disappointments you allow in my children's lives—past, present, and future. Thank you for the sorrows that refine them into pure gold, worthy to be shaped into a crown studded with glittering jewels that you hold in your strong hand.

Give me the wisdom to know when to keep my hands off so you can work in their lives. Show me when and how to step in to discipline or offer help. I rejoice that you never stop calling them to be people who will seek your face and love you with their whole hearts. Thank you that, when they choose to accept you and follow your ways, you view them through the righteousness of your Son. They are beautiful jewels to you, gems you cup in your hands then hold out in victory for all the spiritual powers to view. I bless your holy name for claiming my children as your prized possession and delighting in them.

I pray in Jesus' powerful name, amen.

A mom who knows her children are God's precious gems,

"The Lord will hold you in his hands for all to see—a splendid crown in the hands of God . . . for the Lord delights in you and will claim you as his own." (Isa. 62:3–4)

Further prayer suggestions:

- Praise God now for all he *will* do in the lives of your children, even if you haven't seen it yet.
- List a few ways you believe he will work in your children's lives. Praise him for them.
- Plead with God to continue to make your children more and more like pure gold.
- Ask God to help you see and focus on the precious gemlike qualities in your children.

Day Seven
No Inferiority

Father,

I delight that you look into my children's hearts and love them. Instead of judging them the way people do, you value them by how willingly they soak up the faith you pour out on them. I ask you to help my children learn to view themselves accurately, to evaluate themselves by the depth of their relationship with you.

Don't let the opinions of peers discourage them or give them an inflated notion of their own importance. Don't let them feel inadequate because of things society tells them. Don't even let them judge themselves by the way I treat them, because sometimes I concentrate on their flaws, while other times I see them as more wonderful than they really are.

Please keep feelings of inferiority far from them. When they feel left out or ignored or teased, comfort them with the knowledge that you value them even when people treat them cruelly. Let the mistreatment be an incentive for them to treat others with kindness, while remembering you are the only one they need to please.

When everything they do seems to go well, keep them from arrogance. Remind them how much you hate pride. Impress upon their hearts how little achievements matter if they exalt themselves rather than you. Lead them to humbly thank you for the successes you give them. I pray this in Jesus' holy name, amen.

A mom who believes her children are special,

"I give each of you this warning: Be honest in your estimate of yourselves, measuring your value by how much faith God has given you." (Rom. 12:3)

 101

Further prayer suggestions:

- Ask the Lord to reveal specific places your children may be tempted to feel inferior. Then pray against those temptations.
- Ask the Lord to show you specific times your children have been tempted to pride and then, pray against those tempting times.
- Ask the Lord to reveal to you times you have made your children feel inferior or encouraged them to arrogance and pride. Ask the Lord to forgive you and help you to encourage your children to see themselves through his eyes.

Day Eight
Bless My Children

Heavenly Father,

I know your eyes search the earth continuously, looking for someone to bless. You love my children so much, you *want* to bless them! Anytime their hearts and attitudes are right, you *do* bless them. You bless them with spiritual gifts, you bless them with your friendship, you bless them with comfort when they suffer, and you bless them by promising them a future in heaven. But the sacrifice of your Son on the cross is their greatest blessing.

I also ask for your specific blessings on my children. Please call them to a right relationship with you so that you can fully bless them with no holding back. Help them to grow in wisdom. Bless them with a facility to learn. Show them how to be people who lead others to you. Enable them to do whatever work you provide for them, now and in the future. Bless them with a willingness to work hard to develop natural gifts into skills they can use for you. Bless them with spouses who love you and them. Make them successful in all they do. Allow them to enjoy the gifts you bestow on them.

I thank you for all your blessings, in Jesus' name, amen.

A mom who longs for God to bless her children,

"May the Lord bless you and protect you." (Num. 6:24)

Further prayer and praise suggestions:

- Sometimes we take God's blessings for granted. Ask God to show where he has blessed you or your children that you may not have even noticed. Then thank him profusely.
- Pray for God to bless your children by restoring righteousness to our nation.
- In the space below, write specific blessings you would like to request for your children.

Day Nine
Resisting the Enemy

Jesus,

I praise you because you have given me and my children the power to stay out of Satan's grip. Even though he is a formidable foe who could defeat us easily, you are more powerful than he is. He can do nothing to harm us when we use your mighty name to stand against him. Satan trembles at your name, Jesus. I praise your strong name. You defeated him when you allowed yourself to be sacrificed on the cross to save us. I thank you for your sacrifice. I rejoice with you in your victory over him.

Help my children to understand the importance of humbling themselves in prayer before you so they can tap into your power and build up wisdom and strength to recognize the enemy and resist him. Help them to partner with you in prayer to defeat his plans against them and their friends. Give them confidence in their power to overcome all his schemes by turning to you and speaking your name against the enemy.

Make my children aware of Satan's tactics against them. Give them discernment to recognize his imitations. Reveal every evil plan and give them victory over him. I praise your name, Jesus, that through you my children can and will be victorious over Satan. In Jesus' name I pray, amen.

A mom who knows her children can escape the enemy,

"So humble yourselves before God. Resist the devil, and he will flee from you." (James 4:7)

Further prayer suggestions:

- Ask God to show you any spirit of evil that may harass your child today. Speak the name of that spirit (rebellion, fear, selfishness, lust, etc.) and tell it, in Jesus' name, to leave your child. If you can pray aloud, do so. Say, "In the name of Jesus I *command* the spirit of _____ to leave my child alone. My child belongs to God, and you can't touch him."
- Praise God that he is stronger than your enemy.
- Read Psalm 8:2 and declare that God's enemy is also your children's enemy. Praise God that praise defeats the enemy.
- Ask God to give your children wisdom to see that no human is their enemy—people who oppose them have been duped by the devil. The only enemy is Satan.
- Ask God to lead your children to pray for their enemies.

Day Ten
Choosing Partners

Dear God,

I love being a nurturer and friend to my children. I love helping them mature and grow and learn about you. But the older they get, the more I won't be enough, the more they will need companionship and input from other people, and the more they will have to turn away from me to assert their independence. Lord, I welcome that because I know it is your normal plan of development for them, and I want my children to become healthy adults with healthy relationships.

Thank you for providing a rich variety of people with whom my children can associate and learn. Make my children a light to everyone they meet. But when it comes to their close relationships—roommates, best friends, business partners, and marriage partners—I ask you to show them the importance of teaming up with people who love you. Show them that, eventually, any relationship that does not include you will feel empty. Lead them into relationships with people who will encourage them, uplift them, and hold them responsible for wrong actions. Guide them to friends who will be examples of Christ to them. In return, help my children to stand firm as strong examples to those same friends.

Help them always to value you as the most important friend in their lives. In Jesus' name, amen.

A mom who is grateful for the family of God,

"Don't team up with those who are unbelievers. How can goodness be a partner with wickedness? How can light live with darkness?" (2 Cor. 6:14)

Further prayer suggestions:

- Mention the names of your children's unsaved friends to the Lord and ask him to save them.
- Ask God to make your children willing to wait for the right friends. Help them to realize spending time alone is not the worst thing that can happen to them.
- Pray for them to be patient in waiting for God's chosen mate.

Day Eleven
Promises for My Children

O Lord,

I magnify your name and praise you for stuffing your word full of wonderful promises I can claim for my children. I praise you that they can read the Bible and stand on all your promises for themselves. Give them a full understanding of this wonderful gift. Help them believe they can insert their name in your promises and claim them as their own. Help them to know that every assurance in the Scriptures belongs to them as God's heirs through Jesus Christ the Son. Fill them with faith that, as God's adopted children, they inherit it all. Praise your name!

Give them a desire to memorize your promises so they can pull them into their minds and hearts during difficult times. Remind them there is a promise that deals with every problem they might face. Help them to use your promises to chase away fear and failure, to believe that nothing in all creation can separate them from you, and to know that Satan cannot win against them as long as they trust you.

Give my children a growing understanding of the richness of all you have promised for them. Develop in them hearts full of deep gratitude and make them the kind of people who remember to thank you daily for your promises. I pray in Jesus' name, amen.

A mom who trusts God's promises,

"He has given us all of his rich and wonderful promises. He has promised that you will escape the decadence all around you caused by evil desires . . ." (2 Pet. 1:4)

Further prayer suggestions:

- Search the Word for promises to claim for your children, and then ask the Lord to fulfill those promises in their lives.
- Make a list of promises you have seen the Lord fulfill in your children. Every once in a while, read over it and thank him.

Day Twelve
Chosen

Heavenly Father,

I magnify and praise you for seeing the faces of my children and choosing them to belong to you and serve you before you ever created the world. I praise you that you love them and choose to see them as holy when they accept Christ into their hearts. Even though you know their shortcomings and can look into the blackest parts of their hearts, you choose to see them as righteous. Your generosity completely amazes me—your love for them is so great.

Remind them that you made them fearfully and wonderfully. You embroidered them as a rich tapestry in the womb. You decided who they would be and how they would look. Help them to accept their weaknesses as part of who they are—raw materials for blessings. Don't let them look down on the parts of themselves they don't like and try to hide them, but prompt them to hold those parts up to you, knowing you love them. Help them to willingly give you permission to shape those parts into your image.

Reveal to them the fullness of your love. Help them to accept themselves, knowing they are acceptable to you. Help them to love you so much that they seek to follow you and walk in a way worthy of you. Help them to bless you as *Abba*, Daddy, the Father they love.

A mom who is thankful her children belong to God,

"Long ago, before he even made the world, God loved us and chose us in Christ to be holy and without fault in his eyes." (Eph. 1:4)

Further prayer suggestions:

- Ask the Lord to impact your children with the wonder of being chosen by God.
- Pray for them to seek to please God rather than people.
- If your children have a difficult relationship with their father, pray that God will reveal himself to them as their true Father and show them that earthly parents are not our real parents, just as the earth is not our real home.

Day Thirteen
No Hiding from God

Gracious heavenly Father,

Remind my children every moment of the day, every day of the week, that you see everything they do. They can hide nothing from you, no matter where they are or what time of the day or night it is. Every choice they make is played out in full view of your holy eyes, every unkind word they speak is heard by you, and every unkind action is seen by you. You know every thought.

Let their sins embarrass them. Make them suffer because they are making you view the ugliness of their sins. Make them hate the consequences of wrong actions so much they choose right instead. Let them be aware that you are watching and delighting in the right choices they make.

Set an image of the reality of heaven in their minds and hearts. Help them to remember that someday they will stand before you and you will reward them for every right action they took on earth and ask them to explain every wrong thought, every lazy day. Help them understand how thrilled they will feel for all the good, and how sad they will be for all the times they disappointed you. Keep those things sharp in their minds, Lord. Don't let them fade. In Jesus' name, amen.

A mom who welcomes God's watchful eye,

"Nothing in all creation can hide from him. Everything is naked and exposed before his eyes. This is the God to whom we must explain all that we have done." (Heb. 4:13)

Further prayer suggestions:

- Pray for your children to be thankful God sees everything they do, because it means he is watching over them.
- Pray for your children to think about heaven and the Lord.

Day Fourteen
Avoid Sexual Sin

Gracious heavenly Father,

In a society where illicit sex is accepted as normal and glorified in all the media, my children need protection to remain pure. Help them, Lord, because it is virtually impossible to keep them from peers who view sex outside of marriage as exciting and even expected. Guard their minds and values. Make your ideas their ideas, your standards their standards. Help them to stand firm in the conviction that the sexual relationship is for inside marriage and nowhere else. Lord, protect them!

Sexual temptations are everywhere in our society. Give my children wisdom to understand right from wrong. When temptations come, keep them pure. Help them to draw a firm line.

Keep them from gradually easing into actions that would dishonor you by sinning against their own bodies. Remind them the purpose of dating is to find a mate. Help them to think, "When I marry, how would I feel if my spouse had done this? Would it hurt me or make me jealous?" Give them the strength to refuse to do anything wrong. To *run* from it!

In the name of Jesus, please keep my children pure.

A mom who longs for God's purity,

"Run away from sexual sin! No other sin so clearly affects the body as this one does. For sexual immorality is a sin against your own body." (1 Cor. 6:18)

Further prayer suggestions:

- Ask the Lord to keep the future mates of your children sexually pure.
- Ask the Lord to show you which television and video games to allow and which ones to discourage.

Day Fifteen
No Bullies

Dear Lord,

I don't want my children to be bullies. Give them compassionate hearts that strive to treat others the way they want to be treated. Help them to be kind to others—known for their gentle and gracious spirits. Enable them to see the good in other people, but give them sufficient wisdom to eschew the evil around them.

Protect them from bullies who would see their kindness as weakness and wish to harm them. Protect their bodies from the pain those bullies want to inflict. Protect their spirits and emotions. Help them know how to respond if they are treated badly. Help them endure the hateful words without allowing the accusations to enter their hearts. Let them be examples of Jesus.

Help them recognize the changing forms bullying can take as they grow older. Make them refuse to make cruel jokes at others' expense. Keep them from sarcasm and all other put-down language. Make them encouragers whose words delight the people around them.

I ask these things in Jesus' name, amen.

A mom who wants kind, considerate children,

"Be kind to each other." (Ep. 4:32) "Do for others what you would like them to do for you." (Matt. 7:12)

Further prayer suggestions:

- Pray for God to protect your children's friends from bullies.
- Ask the Lord to give your children courage if they are bullied.
- Pray for them to have the courage to defend younger and weaker children.

Day Sixteen
Finding God's Will

O God,

I magnify you because you want the best for my children. Thank you that you are able to work out every circumstance in their lives for their greatest good and your greatest good. Thank you that if they seek your will, they will find it. You *will* direct their paths. And you can send more blessings than they can even imagine.

Help them to know nothing is too small for you. Call them to seek your will in everything they undertake—little or large. When they awaken in the morning, lead them to ask what you have for them to do that day. During the day, help them to constantly ask, "Is that what you want me to do, Lord?" Help them search your Word for wisdom in prioritizing every action.

Open the right doors for them and close the wrong ones. Show them that as long as they are trusting you with all their hearts and depending on you, you will guide them. Help them understand that as long as they seek hard after you, they are free to do the things that seem desirable to them—because you are constantly placing right desires in their hearts so you can grant them. In Jesus' name, amen.

A mom who wants God's will for her children,

"Seek his will in all you do, and he will direct your paths." (Prov. 3:6)

Further prayer suggestions:

- Pray for your children to have faith that the Lord intends to lead them into his will for them.
- Pray for them to *want* his will—no matter what.
- Ask the Lord to keep them from impatience. Ask him to keep them from trying to rush into things before they hear from him.

Day Seventeen
Temptation

Dear heavenly Father,

Thank you for your incredible love for my children. Thank you for giving them the tools to overcome temptation. Thank you for letting them know that the way of escape is to *run* from it. Fast!

Protect them from the evil in this world. Give my children the maturity to instantly recognize it and reject it. Help them to recognize that if they toy with evil it will overcome them. When temptation comes, help them to immediately clear their minds of any impure thoughts and replace them with thoughts that are pure. Make evil as disgusting to them as rotting flesh. Give them the courage to remove themselves physically and mentally from it the first chance they get—no matter what everyone else is doing. No matter what anyone else will think of them. Help them stand up and walk away, knowing that God always makes a way to escape.

Give them right attitudes so they will desire to pursue activities that increase their faith and make them righteous. Bless them with hearts that delight to do good and not evil. I ask this in Jesus' name, amen.

A caring mom,

"Run from anything that stimulates youthful lust. Follow anything that makes you want to do right." (2 Tim. 2:22)

Further prayer suggestions:

- In the space below, write out any specific needs or problems to pray over for your children today. Later, when God answers the prayer, write down the answer and date.

Day Eighteen
Hate Evil

Father God,

I praise you for making it possible for my children to discern the difference between right and wrong. I know some societies have fallen so far from you they no longer are able to recognize evil. Instead they embrace it. Don't let that happen to us. Reveal to my children how society flips values, claiming evil is good and good is evil. Don't let my children be fooled. Give them the maturity to recognize evil. Instill in them an intense hatred for evil.

Don't let my children buy into the philosophy that calls anyone who takes a stand against evil a hate monger or a bigot. Give them backbones of bronze and make them eager to take a strong stand against evil. Show them that it *is* possible to hate the sin and love the sinner. Give them compassion and love for people duped by sin— while protecting them from falling into the same sin themselves. Let them feel sad for the person choosing to do evil, but don't allow them to excuse evil or have compassion on evil. Help them understand Satan is the enemy; the people he tricks are not the enemy.

Make evil repulsive to my children. Urge them to reject it. Make them always courageous, unafraid to speak out against evil, never ashamed to stand for righteousness. Help them to hate evil and choose purity. In Jesus' name, amen.

A mom who loves the Lord and hates evil,

"You who love the Lord, hate evil!" (Ps. 97:10)

Further prayer suggestions:

- Pray for God to give your children eloquent words to explain any stance they take against evil.
- Ask the Lord to help them find favor in the eyes of people so they can influence many lives for good.

Day Nineteen
Addictions

Dear Lord,

I praise you for freeing my children from slavery to Satan and sin. How wonderful that when my children choose to obey you, blessings and joy flood their lives because you become their master. And you lead them into bright futures filled with success and happiness.

But, heavenly Father, it is so easy for my children to slide into the temptation of choosing to love *things* rather than you. Don't let them becomes slaves to the things the world offers. Don't let them become addicted to sexual stimulants, drugs, alcohol, lying, pornography, video games, the Internet, or anything else. O, Lord, the list is so long. Keep them from becoming addicted to friends by caring too much what their friends think and too little what you think.

In the strong name of Jesus, I come against the spirit of addiction, and I tell it to stay away from my children. Help them recognize wrong priorities before those things become addictions; make them hate and avoid obvious evil. Protect them by filling their legitimate needs and helping them choose you first in their lives. Thank you. I believe you will do all these things. In Jesus' name, amen.

A mom who knows God protects her children,

"Don't you realize that whatever you choose to obey becomes your master?" (Rom. 7:16)

Further prayer suggestions:

- List as many needs as you can think of, then ask God to fill those needs in your children.
- Ask God to keep their future spouses from all addiction.
- Ask the Lord to help you recognize if any of your children start down the path to addiction, then pray specifically against their particular addiction.

❧ Day Twenty
Inner Peace

Dear God,

I praise you that your peace is available for my children. Thank you that my children can turn to you and escape despair. Show them how to take every problem to you in prayer the second it pops into their thoughts. Help them to tell you what they need, then fix their minds on pure, lovely things. Help them remember all the blessings in their lives and thank you. Fill them with your joy. Grant them faith to trust that you will guide them to solutions and make their paths straight before them.

Keep them from worry. When schoolwork seems too difficult, help them to tell you about it and then turn to study. If they are overlooked for awards or sports teams or plays, call them to pour out their disappointment to you. Then help them understand that you use those disappointments to shape character and divert them onto new paths. Help them to ask you for help in difficult relationships, then care more about pleasing you than their friends.

Make them positive people who think about true, honorable, and right things rather than focusing on the negative. Fulfill your promise to grant them peace that passes human understanding. In Jesus' name, amen.

A mom who appreciates God's comforting love,

"Don't worry about anything; instead, pray about everything. Tell God what you need, and thank him for what he has done." (Phil. 4:6)

❧ 127

Further prayer suggestions:

- Take your time and pray the entire Philippians 4:4–14 passage for your children and yourself.
- During the rest of the day, praise God for the peace he will give you and your children when you follow these directions.

Day Twenty-One
Angel Protection

Dear heavenly Father,

Gratitude overwhelms me when I think my children are such a treasure to you that you send angels to protect them. You dispatch your mighty ones to shield my children with their wings and hold them in their hands—protecting them from harm, standing between them and the evil one. Thank you, Lord.

I ask you to send your ministering angels to surround them today. Keep them from physical abuse, rape, attack, or abduction. Guard them and keep them from accidental injury. Guard their brains, bones, and organs during sporting events. Guard them from danger I have no idea how to anticipate. Keep evil people intent on harm away from them.

Thank you that you have always been the one protecting them, even when I imagined it was my careful mothering. I am so grateful that you are their true parent and you only lent them to me for a while. So no matter whether they are in my home or across the country, they are just as safe as when I held them in my arms as infants— because you and your angels are watching over them. In Jesus' name, I thank you, amen.

A grateful mom,

"For he orders his angels to protect you wherever you go." (Ps. 91:11)

Further prayer suggestions:

- Thank God for all the times he protected your children when you were not even aware of danger.
- Thank the Lord because he works out for good any injury or problem he allows into their lives.

Day Twenty-Two
Biting and Devouring

Heavenly Father,

I praise you because you are a God of love and you have commanded my children to love others as they love themselves. I thank you for making your laws simple. So simple that if they totally succeed in acting in love toward others, they won't do anything to offend you or anyone else. I praise you because love sums up all your laws. You *are* love.

Please forgive my children for the times selfishness creeps in and they treat others with disrespect or contempt. Change their hearts. Take away the feeling that everyone is wrong except those in their own little group. Help them to grow deep into your love so they are not even tempted to injure others with words. Keep my children from unkind teasing that tears down friends. Help them refuse to criticize or slander because they understand how the result of hurtful talk can destroy friends and family members.

Guard their hearts so that unfair criticism aimed at them doesn't wound them. Convince them that they are valuable to you no matter what anyone else says to them. Help them welcome constructive criticism so they can grow from it. I ask in Jesus' name, amen.

A mom who desires godly children,

"But if instead of showing love among yourselves you are always biting and devouring one another, watch out! Beware of destroying one another." (Gal. 5:15)

Further prayer suggestions:

- Pray through Galatians 5:13–26. Spend extra time praying verses twenty-two and twenty-three into your children.
- In the name of Jesus, stand against all the evils mentioned in verses nineteen to twenty-one. Thank God he can keep them from those things.

Day Twenty-Three
Bearing Fruit

Almighty God,

I extol you because you are the vine and my children, the branches, pull nourishment from you. As long as they remain in you through Bible reading and prayer they *will* bear fruit. You promised they would and you always fulfill your promises. Thank you, Father.

Thank you for always being there for them, holding them up, and feeding them. Help them to cling to you, to hang on for dear life and then recognize the fruit you bring forth. Produce the fruit of faithfulness in them. Give them love, joy, peace, patience, kindness, gentleness, and self-control. Make them determined to let those fruits shine forth as they walk through doors you open for them and down paths you point them toward.

Make them satisfied with wherever you send them and whatever you give them. Make them bloom where they are planted. Make them content as ordinary human beings with ordinary jobs. Show them that any work done with all their might will glorify you—even the lowliest job—as long as they rest in you, allowing you to produce fruit in them. Make them content with C grades if that is the best they can do. But help them to welcome fame and fortune if that is your choice for them. In Jesus' name, amen.

A mom who cares deeply,

"Those who remain in me, and I in them, will produce much fruit. For apart from me you can do nothing." (John 15:5)

Further prayer suggestions:

- Pray for your children to understand that God is responsible to produce fruit through them. They don't need to fret about it.
- Ask God to show them that fruit is a guarantee if they stay close to the Lord. They don't need to worry about anything but obeying him and seeking his face.
- Thank God that he will reward them in heaven for the fruit they bear now.

Day Twenty-Four
Prayers Answered

Gracious Father,

I thank you that you welcome and answer my children's prayers. Make them people of prayer. When trouble comes, give them a strong desire to turn to you instead of relying on their own strength. Help them learn to ask you to fill their needs. Help them to bring requests for friends and family to you. Make them understand that nothing is too small to bring to you.

I praise you for Jesus' promise that every single prayer they send up to you *is* answered. Help them believe that if they ask, you answer. Always. Keep them asking, over and over, until they hear from you. Help them to continue knocking on the door of prayer, even when the answer seems impossible, because the door opens to everyone who knocks. Help them believe you have all power and can do anything. Give them faith to believe that even when the answer may not be the one expected or wanted, they can know it is the best answer for them—because you give only good gifts.

Help them to recognize the answers when you send them. Increase their faith as they see the wonders of answered prayer. Help them to develop a relationship with you through prayer. In times when they can't feel your presence in prayer, give them the faith to believe that you are listening. And answering. In Jesus' name, amen.

A mom who knows God answers prayer,

"For everyone who asks, receives. Everyone who seeks, finds. And the door is opened to everyone who knocks." (Matt. 7:8)

Further prayer suggestions:

- Ask the Lord to help you become an example of a praying person to your children.
- Ask God to make them examples of praying people to their peers.
- Pray for them to draw closer and closer to God through prayer. Ask the Lord to give them a relationship with him few achieve until they are old.

Day Twenty-Five
Future Plans

Dear God,

I praise you that you have a marvelous future in store for my children. Thank you that you are so kind and good you would never harm them. And you have the power to shape them into anything you want them to be. You can give them whatever job you want for them and the skills they need to accomplish your purposes. Thank you for planning a multitude of good works for them to complete in their lives—helpful deeds and words to encourage people. Thank you that they will be amply rewarded on earth by seeing a few of the results of those good works, and you will reward them beyond measure in heaven some day.

Fulfill your plans in their lives. Help them to always seek your face so you can communicate your plans to them and lead them. Help them to stay close to you and give you permission to fill them with your Spirit so they will qualify for the great plans you have for them.

Thank you that when trials come, my children can always hope in you, knowing you will guide them and protect them and fulfill your specific plan for each of them. In Jesus' name, amen.

A mom who believes God has a
wonderful plan for each of her children,

"'For I know the plans I have for you,' says the Lord. 'They are plans for good and not for disaster, to give you a future and a hope'." (Jer. 29:11)

Further prayer suggestions:

- Pray for God to strengthen the abilities he has given your children so they will be more effective in their chosen fields.
- Ask God to let your children bless others as he works out his plan for them.

Day Twenty-Six
Fall into Line

Mighty God,

I magnify you because you are omniscient. You know exactly what my children should do and how they should behave to lead successful contented lives. Help them to trust you in that. Prove to them that when your instructions seem to contradict common sense—common sense is off track. You're smarter than they are. Your ways are higher than their ways. Your thoughts are as numerous as the grains of sand on the beach. They sometimes have a twisted view of right and wrong—you never do.

Make my children believe in you with such vehemence that they never fight your instructions. Inspire them to study your ways. Then the instant they see a point where their path diverges from your Word, help them fall into line with you. Lead them to base their daily actions on what your Word tells them you want them to do. Give them faith to eventually understand how your instructions were correct. Help them praise you for allowing them to follow you.

Make them examples of obedient godly people to their peers. Help friends to see the way they follow you and long to be just like them. In Jesus' name I pray, amen.

A mom who longs for godly children,

"Notice the way God does things; then fall into line. Don't fight the ways of God, for who can straighten out what he has made crooked?" (Eccles. 7:13)

Further prayer suggestions:

- Pray for your children to spend time in the Bible so they know how to fall into line with how God wants them to behave.
- Pray that they will never be ashamed to explain to others how much they want to follow the Lord.

Day Twenty-Seven
Avoid Wrong Teaching

Heavenly Father,

I thank you for giving my children the opportunity to know the truth. Thank you for writing your thoughts and laws in the Bible. Thank you that my children can figure out solutions to problems by reading it and applying the wisdom they find in its pages. Thank you that by diligence in studying it, they can keep from getting mixed up and behaving in destructive ways that would hurt them and make them feel ashamed later.

But I know that as they get older, sometimes they don't stay in the Word as they should. And they begin to listen to friends and teachers who convincingly set forth wrong, harmful ideas and theories.

Lord, don't let that happen! I beg you to keep my children from deception. Let them be so full of you and your Word that *they* will be the persuasive speakers in any conversation. Instead of others changing them, let my children lead those people to you. Give them clear minds to remember and repeat your logical truths. Keep them from confusion. Help them reject books and movies that would lead them from you. Keep them strong, firmly planted in you like an oak whose roots grow deep. I ask this in Jesus' name, amen.

A mom who wants her children to know
and obey God's Word,

"And many false prophets will appear and will lead many people astray . . . But those who endure to the end will be saved." (Matt. 24:11–13)

Further prayer suggestions:

- Ask the Lord to give your children a strong desire to read the Bible.
- Pray for the Holy Spirit to give them understanding as they read.
- Ask the Lord to give them wisdom to always discern his truth.

I
No Co

Gracious
What
heavy bur
hearts the
are dead t
to you. N
eous thro
Help
sneak in
inferiorit
him a liar
for them
and wortl
for him a
Let tl
surround
demnation
ous name

"So now th

Day Twenty-Eight
Love Others

Gracious heavenly Father,

I praise you that you are a God of love. Thank you that you are holy and righteous and you want my children to be like you—you want them to love others the way you love them. Give them eyes to see the world through your eyes of love. Forgive them for the many times they fall short. Thank you for accepting them, despite their tendencies to be unloving, as you lead them closer to your perfect love.

Thank you for helping John make it clear how wrong it is to hate fellow Christians, because you live in them and we are all part of one body. I praise you for understanding how Christians may hurt my children, either inadvertently or because ideas are twisted. And my children may do the same to fellow Christians. Thank you for your willingness to forgive them all and make them right with each other and you again.

Remind them love is an *action*, not a *feeling*. Help them act in love toward the people who wrong them. Give them wisdom to overlook flaws. Help them pray for other Christians rather than resenting them. Help them bless rather than curse. Pull up any bitter roots that try to grip their hearts, and wind the tendrils of your love around them instead. In Jesus' precious name I pray, amen.

A mom who loves God and her children,

"This is the message we have heard from the beginning: We should love one another."
(*1 John 3:11*)

Further prayer suggestions:

- Pray for your children to accept the Lord if they haven't already done so.
- Pray for them to hold onto a picture of themselves as new creations in Christ.
- Ask the Lord to dim any memories you have of ways your children have disappointed you. Ask him to give you a fresh, new vision of them covered with his righteousness.

Day Thirty
Praise for Weakness

Dear loving Abba Father,

I praise you that my children are imperfect! I ask you to show them what a privilege it is to make mistakes and be inadequate, because that gives you a chance to show how great you are through them. Humble them so that you can lift them up and shine your power through them. Make them thrill to let you claim all the glory.

Help them to thank you for the times when, like Moses, they stutter and the words won't come. Help them to be grateful when they're shy or lack skill in a sporting event or can't understand math concepts—when they aren't fast enough or smart enough. Those are the times your strength is made perfect in their weakness. When you use them despite their inadequacies, let people recognize it must be you working through them.

I pray that inside their hearts and heads they never *feel* inferior because they belong to you. Help them feel like a garden fountain—standing, while you flow through them to bless others. In Jesus' name, amen.

A mom standing in God's glorious strength,

"Each time he said, 'My gracious favor is all you need. My power works best in your weakness.'" (2 Cor. 12:9)

Further prayer suggestions:

- Think of the specific weaknesses of your children and thank God he will work despite them, through them, to show himself strong in your children.
- Pray for your children to view their shortcomings through God's eyes

Day Thirty-One
Tender Conscience

Dear God,

I magnify you, because when my children do wrong you speak to them through their consciences. Give them tender consciences. Give them hearts that long to do right. Make them quick to admit when they are wrong. Squash big egos if they arise. Keep them from the stubbornness that leads to trouble by preventing them from admitting they are wrong. Keep them from trying to cover their sins so they look better to others. Prevent them from striking out at others to defend themselves.

Show them that looking smart or important on the outside doesn't mean anything; godly heart attitudes give them value to you and others. Show them that any sin against others is against you first. When they do wrong, prick their consciences; let their own self-talk accuse them and make them miserable. Help them to understand that the purpose of a guilty conscience is to make them sorry for sin so they will repent and change. Help them to immediately confess because they know you see them as they really are and they want to be right with you. Make them willing to submit to your authority. In Jesus' name I pray, amen.

A loving mom,

"Blessed are those who have a tender conscience, but the stubborn are headed for serious trouble." (Prov. 29:14)

Further prayer suggestions:

- In the strong name of Jesus, come against the spirits of rebellion, ego, and stubbornness that may exist in your children.
- Ask God to show you how to discipline in ways that discourage those attitudes from ever taking up residence in them.

Extra #1
Finding the Right Mate

Dear Lord,

How grateful I am that you have chosen my children for you. Help them rest in the knowledge that you are in the process of preparing a mate who will complete them by loving them and spurring them on to love you more and serve you better. At this very moment, you are shaping a spouse who will complement them—fit their personalities and bodies. Give my children great faith in that truth. Help them not to worry and hurry to find a mate.

Help them welcome any loneliness as correction from you. Let them invite it to strengthen them and make them like pure gold for you and their future spouse. Keep them from feelings of inferiority if they are not pursued by the opposite sex. Make them strong enough to say no if they are.

Lord, show them how to spend this time deepening their relationship with you and developing their skills. Show them how to make the most of their time. Help them enjoy learning and working at making themselves the best they can be for you and the mate you will send them. I ask all these things for my children and for their future spouses in Jesus' name, amen.

A mom who believes God has a great future for her children,

"And the Lord God said, 'It is not good for man to be alone. I will make a companion who will help him.'" (Genesis 2:18)

Further prayer suggestions:

- Pray against impatience in your children when they begin to search for a mate.
- List some specific spiritual qualities you want in your children's future spouses and pray for them through the day.

Extra #2
Walk Worthy

Lord,

I glorify and exalt your name, because you are able to make my children worthy of the life to which you called them. You are able to fulfill all the plans you have for them. You are able to keep them pure and full of love for others. You are able to expose all Satan's imitations and keep my children from being fooled and destroyed by him. Praise your powerful name!

Please grant them a fervent desire to walk in a way worthy of you— to bring you pleasure and delight. Fill their hearts with determination to serve you and love others; then fulfill those good intentions for them. Keep them faithful in everything. Show them that when they are faithful, you will produce fruit in them. You will make their walk worthy.

Thank you for choosing my family for adoption into your family. Inspire me to continue faithfully in prayer for my children until my life ends and I go to heaven to be with you. In Jesus' name, amen.

A mom who knows God can make
her children pleasing in his sight,

"And so we keep on praying for you, that our God will make you worthy of the life to which he called you. And we pray that God, by his power, will fulfill all your good intentions and faithful deeds." (2 Thess. 1:11)

Further prayer suggestions:

- Ask the Lord to make your walk worthy so you can be an example to your children.
- Invite the spirit of purity to fill your children.

Extra #3
Respect for Authority

Dear God,

I praise you for instituting authorities to protect my children and hold them accountable. Thank you for the parents you gave to me as my authorities, even though they were imperfect. Thank you for allowing me to guide and discipline my own children, even though I make mistakes. Help me to overlook the faults in my parents as you help my children forgive me for mine. Keep them from being damaged by the flawed decisions I sometimes make, and give me wisdom to make better choices.

Take the spirit of rebellion from my children. Help small children to submit to my authority as their parent and older children to listen to my ideas with respect. Lead them to finish assigned work at school or in their jobs without complaint. Help them understand that the people over them may make mistakes, but those people were put in authority by you, and if my children choose to disregard or disobey them, they are rebelling against you.

If they see evil in the government, give them courage to speak out against the wrongs without trying to usurp your right for vengeance. Help them to act with graciousness and wisdom as your representatives. If they need to confront sinful authorities, give them gentle, quiet spirits supported by backbones of steel. I ask this in Jesus' name, amen.

A mom who submits to God's authority,

"Everyone must submit himself to the governing authorities, for there is no authority except that which God has established." (Rom. 13:1 NIV)

Further prayer suggestions:

- Confess any spirit of rebellion in yourself. Ask God to remove it and protect your children from following the bad example you set for them in the past.
- In the name of Jesus, command any spirit of rebellion to leave your children.

Section Four

Carry-Along Prayer Cards

Carry-Along Prayer Cards

The abridgement of your daily prayers can be cut from these pages and pasted or taped to a three-by-five inch index card. Take the card with you wherever you go—place it in your purse, place it on the refrigerator door, or tape it to the bathroom mirror as a reminder of your daily prayer for your children.

(cut along dotted lines)

....

Day One: My Children Can Delight God

Lord, help my children to give you pleasure by seeking you with all their hearts, minds, and souls.

....

Day Two: Forgiveness

Heavenly Father, call my children to turn to you for forgiveness the instant they sin. Give them faith to know their sins are forgiven.

....

✑ Day Three: Forgiving Others

God, remove all bitterness and resentment from my children and give them forgiving hearts.

✑ Day Four: Attending Church

Dear Jesus, lead my children to a good, solid church with righteous leaders where they can use their gifts and grow closer to you.

✑ Day Five: Good Work Habits

Lord, help my children work hard and cheerfully at whatever they do—because they want to do their best for you.

✑ Day Six: My Treasure—God's Treasure

Dear Lord, shape my children into beautiful jewels sparkling in your hand. Help them delight you.

✑ Day Seven: No Inferiority

Heavenly Father, teach my children to measure themselves by how much faith they have in you. Keep them from arrogance or inferiority. Give them confidence.

ᐧ Day Eight: Bless My Children

Abba Father, I know you can and will bless and protect my children today. Thank you.

ᐧ Day Nine: Resisting the Enemy

Jesus, help my children to recognize and resist the devil when he attacks. Praise you that when they resist him, he will flee.

ᐧ Day Ten: Choosing Partners

God, lead my children to companions who love you and will draw them into a closer relationship with you.

ᐧ Day Eleven: Promises for My Children

Jesus, give my children an understanding of the richness of your promises. Help them claim the promises as their own.

ᐧ Day Twelve: Chosen

Heavenly Father, help my children understand you chose them for yourself even before you created the world. Make them feel loved and special because you value them.

Day Thirteen: No Hiding from God

Gracious Father, give my children a constant awareness that you lovingly watch everything they do. Let that motivate them to do their best and stay pure.

Day Fourteen: Avoid Sexual Sin

Lord, don't let my children be influenced by this evil society. Keep them sexually pure—even in their thoughts.

Day Fifteen: No Bullies

Heavenly Father, help my children treat others the way they want to be treated.

Day Sixteen: Finding God's Will

Dear God, help my children put you ahead of everything and everyone, so you can lead them in the right direction and reveal your will for them.

Day Seventeen: Temptation

Lord, help my children run from anything that stimulates lust. Encourage them to follow things that make them want to do right.

ᕱ Day Eighteen: Hate Evil

Jesus, help my children to love people and hate evil.

ᕱ Day Nineteen: Addictions

Lord, protect my children from every addiction. Make them slaves to you rather than to sin.

ᕱ Day Twenty: Inner Peace

God, keep my children from worry. Help them to simply tell you what they need, then thank you for answering their prayer. Give them peace.

ᕱ Day Twenty-One: Angel Protection

Dear Lord, send your mighty angels to spread protecting wings around my children. Keep their hearts, minds, and bodies safe.

ᕱ Day Twenty-Two: Biting and Devouring

Father, make my children kind and considerate toward others. Protect their spirits when others criticize them unfairly or ridicule them.

Day Twenty-Three: Bearing Fruit

Lord, make my children abide in you through Bible reading and prayer so they can bear much fruit. Use them in your kingdom.

Day Twenty-Four: Prayers Answered

Father, give my children great confidence in the power of prayer. Make them people who pray and keep asking until you answer.

Day Twenty-Five: Future Plans

Dear God, help my children remember you have great things in store for them. Keep them walking with you so you can fulfill those plans in their lives.

Day Twenty-Six: Fall into Line

Lord, help my children to notice the way you want things done and then to fall into line. Help them never to fight your ways, but to recognize them as best.

Day Twenty-Seven: Avoid Wrong Teaching

God, don't let false teaching lead my children astray. Keep their faith in you strong.

Day Twenty-Eight: Love Others

Gracious heavenly Father, help my children please you by loving your people.

Day Twenty-Nine: No Condemnation

Jesus, help my children understand that there is no condemnation for them because they accepted you. Help them to recognize and reject all false guilt.

Day Thirty: Praise for Weakness

Heavenly Father, don't let my children wallow in inferiority and insecurity. Help them to see their weaknesses as an opportunity for your strength to be seen through them.

Day Thirty-One: Tender Conscience

Dear Lord, keep my children from stubbornness. Give them tender consciences.

✑ Extra #1: Finding the Right Mate

God, help my children grow closer to you as they wait for the mate you are preparing for them.

✑ Extra #2: Walk Worthy

Dear Lord, make my children worthy of the life to which you have called them.

✑ Extra #3: Respect for Authority

Cleanse my children of any spirit of rebellion and make them willing to submit to your authority.